Peterson First Guide to Butterflies and Moths

Paul A. Opler

Illustrated by
Amy Bartlett Wright

HOUGHTON MIFFLIN COMPANY
Boston New York

Library of Congress Cataloging-in-Publication Data

Opler, Paul A.
Peterson first guide to butterflies and moths/Paul A.
Opler; illustrated by Amy Bartlett Wright.
p. cm.
"Text based on Field guide to eastern butterflies by
Paul Opler, copyright 1992" — T.p. verso.
Includes index.
ISBN 0-395-67072-1
1. Lepidoptera — North America — Identification. I.
Opler, Paul A. Field guide to eastern butterflies.
II. Title.
QL548.064 1994
595.78'0973 — dc20 93-5751
CIP

Printed in Italy

NWI 10 9 8 7 6 5 4 3 2

Editor's Note

In 1934, my *Field Guide to the Birds* first saw the light of day. This book was designed so that live birds could be readily identified at a distance, by their patterns, shapes, and field marks, without resorting to the technical points specialists use to name species in the hand or in the specimen tray. The book introduced the "Peterson System," as it is now called, a visual system based on patternistic drawings with arrows to pinpoint the key field marks. The system is now used throughout the Peterson Field Guide Series, which has grown to nearly 50 volumes on a wide range of nature subjects, from ferns to fishes, rocks to stars, animal tracks to edible plants.

Even though Peterson Field Guides are intended for the novice as well as the expert, there are still many beginners who would like something even simpler to start with — a smaller guide that would give them confidence. It is for this audience — those who perhaps recognize a crow or a robin, buttercup or daisy, but little else — that the Peterson First Guides have been created. They offer a selection of the animals and plants you are most likely to see during your first forays afield. By narrowing the choices — and using the Peterson System — First Guides make it easier to get started and to graduate to the full-fledged Peterson Field Guides.

Butterflies and moths are becoming increasingly popular. Gardening to attract butterflies, butterfly watching, and butterfly conservation are drawing the attention of thousands. This small book, written with authority by Paul A. Opler and illustrated so skillfully by Amy Bartlett Wright, is designed as an introduction to some of the most common and noteworthy of the more than 800 butterflies and the more than 12,000 kinds of moths that grace our continent.

Roger Tory Peterson

Introducing the Butterflies and Moths

This small book introduces 182 of the 800 butterflies and several thousand moths found in North America. All the most common and notable species are included — all those you are most likely to see in the field. After you have become familiar with the common species, you may want to go on to some of the reference books listed in the back of this guide.

What's the Difference Between a Butterfly and a Moth?

This question has an easy, but not completely true, answer: Butterflies fly during the day, are brightly colored, have clubbed antennae, and rest with their wings held up together.

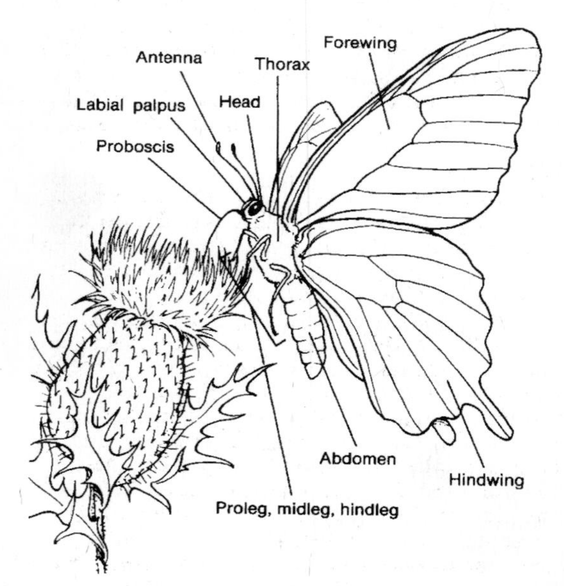

Parts of a butterfly's body.

Moths mostly fly at night, are mostly dull in color, rest with their wings folded tentlike over their back, and have a *frenulum*, a wing-coupling mechanism that allows the forewing and hindwing to move together in flight. But some butterflies fly at night, some moths fly during the day, some butterflies lack clubbed antennae, some moths hold their wings up like butterflies, and of course there are many dull-colored butterflies and some very colorful moths.

Butterflies and moths together make up the order of insects called the Lepidoptera (*lepido*=scale, *pteros*=wing). Like most insects, butterflies and moths have three main body parts: head, thorax, and abdomen. On the head are two compound eyes; two antennae, which are used for smell and balance; and the proboscis, used to take in fluids such as flower nectar and juices from ripe fruit. On the thorax are the two pairs of wings — forewings and hindwings — and three pairs of legs. The wings are covered with overlapping rows of tiny scales. The strong muscles inside the thorax move the thorax and the wings and legs. Inside the abdomen are the vital organs; at the end of the abdomen are the structures used in mating.

Life Cycle

All butterflies and moths have four life stages — the egg, the caterpillar or larva, the pupa, and the adult. Less advanced insects, such as aphids and grasshoppers, have only three life stages — egg, nymph, and adult.

After mating, the female lays her eggs on or near a "host plant," a plant the caterpillars will eat. The eggs may hatch within a few days, but the eggs of some species can survive for months or even years until conditions are right for the larvae. After the eggs hatch, the tiny caterpillars begin to eat. As they grow, they molt or shed their skin several times. When they are ready to pupate, they search out a sheltered spot and then shed their skin one last time to reveal the pupa, or chrysalis. The pupae of many moths and a few butterflies are enclosed in a silk bag made by the caterpillar, but the chrysalids of most butterflies are naked. Inside the chrysalis, the structures of the caterpillar are broken down and dissolved, and the adult structures develop. After the transformation is complete, the adult butterfly or moth emerges, pumps fluid to expand its wings, and then begins the cycle anew.

How to Study Butterflies and Moths

You can begin to study butterflies and moths just by observing them. You might also want to try photographing the insects. Later on, you may want to start a collection of your own.

To watch butterflies and moths, first find a good habitat near your home or school (see

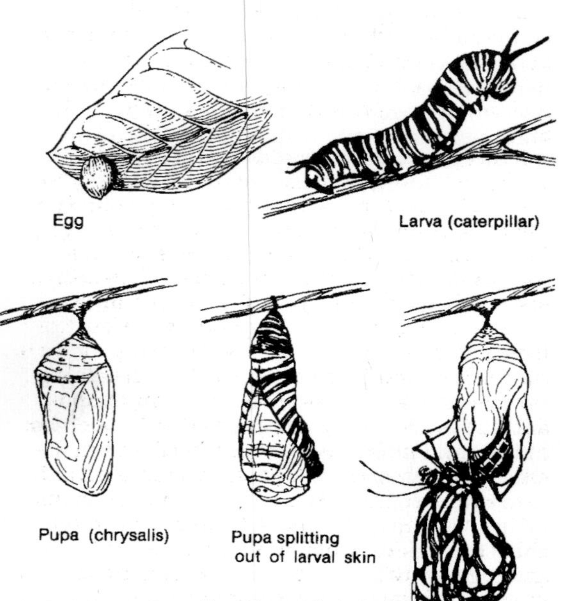

Life cycle of a Monarch butterfly.

Habitats on page 8). Go out during the day, and take along this book, a notebook, and a net or close-focus binoculars. Select one individual butterfly or moth and observe it as long as you can. Watch it to see what it does. Does it drink nectar at flowers or feed on fermenting fruit or tree sap? Does it lay eggs or engage in courtship with the opposite sex? Or does it just seem to be resting or sunning?

Of course you wlll see only a few moths in the daytime. To find more moths, go out at night and use a light or bait to attract them.

By keeping good notes for a long period of time, you will gain a good understanding of common butterflies and moths. You will learn about their feeding and mating habits, about what kind of habitats they seem to use most, and what times of year each species is on the wing.

Photographing butterflies and moths is tricky but rewarding; it is an excellent way to build a "collection" without harming your specimens. For the best results, you should use a 35mm camera with a close-up lens and an electronic flash. I recommend color film with a speed of between 64 and 200. Go out in the early morning or late afternoon, when butterflies and moths are less active. When you see a butterfly or moth you want to photograph, approach it slowly, without letting your shadow fall on the insect. Be patient and still; take the picture when the insect is centered and in focus. I usually take more than one photograph to make sure that I have at least one good one.

The right way to make a butterfly or moth collection is described in more advanced guides. You will need a net, a killing jar, a spreading board, and one or more soft-bottomed boxes in which to keep your specimens. You can make these items or buy them from a biological equipment supplier. Before you start a collection, make sure that you are committed to it, because you must take care of your specimens. It would be a shame to kill insects for your collection and then let the specimens be destroyed by carelessness.

When collecting, remember not to trespass on private land without permission. Collecting in national and state parks, wildlife refuges, and nature preserves is usually prohibited.

Raising Butterflies and Moths

A good way to get to know butterflies and moths intimately is to raise them from caterpillars or eggs. You can watch and photograph all the life stages, and have the pleasure of releasing the adult after it emerges.

You can raise butterflies and moths either by finding eggs or caterpillars or by putting a female in a screen cage with its caterpillar food plant (consult a Field Guide or the *First Guide to Caterpillars* to find out what plants each caterpillar eats). After the eggs hatch, the small caterpillars must be kept in a suitable container and given shelter and plenty of fresh food. Make sure no pesticides have been used on the food you give your "livestock"! The container must be kept clean to avoid mold or diseases, and the temperature and moisture level must be comfortable for that species.

When the caterpillars near full size, make sure they have a place to pupate. Most butterflies need to hang their chrysalids from a stick or piece of bark; many moths form cocoons in loose soil or leaf litter.

Keep a close eye on your pupae as the time nears for them to emerge. The adults will need enough room to hang and let their wings spread, expand, and dry. After their wings have hardened, you can photograph them in your garden and then release them.

Habitats

A habitat is the home environment of an animal or plant. Each kind of butterfly and moth has its own unique habitat that has all the necessary elements for its lifestyle. These include nectar plants or other foods for adults, caterpillar food plants, mating or courtship areas, and possibly roosting areas. If you want to find a particular butterfly or moth, be sure you know what its requirements are so that you can look in the right habitat.

Zebra Swallowtails, for example, live in moist

river woodlands in the eastern United States, where they can find pawpaw, their caterpillar host plant, flowers for nectar, and mating arenas. On the other hand, the Douglas-fir Tussock Moth is found in western coniferous forests where its caterpillar host plants, firs and Douglas-fir, are found.

Try to visit as many kinds of habitats as possible to find the maximum variety of butterflies and moths. One way to divide habitats is into forests, wetlands, and open areas. Each of these groups can be divided into smaller groups. Forests can be classified by the different kinds of dominant trees: conifers or deciduous trees, oak or maple. Wetlands include marshes, bogs, rivers, streams, and swamps. Open areas include meadows, farmland, gardens, roadsides, and dunes. Make lists of the butterflies and moths that you find in each kind of habitat.

Gardening to Attract Butterflies and Moths

An excellent way to attract butterflies and moths to your yard is to plant nectar plants and caterpillar host plants. The kinds of plants will depend on the region you live in and the species found in your neighborhood.

You should provide nectar plants or other foods for adults, the plants on which the females lay their eggs and the caterpillars feed, and places for sheltering and roosting. Remember to include nectar plants for each season so that there will be a sequence of flowering from spring to fall. Also remember that different species use different nectar plants. Many of these nectar plants are listed in the species descriptions in this book.

Commonly used butterfly nectar plants include buddleia, marigold, zinnia, lilac, lantana, butterfly milkweed, asters, and mints. Moths use night-flowering plants that are fragrant and pale-colored. These include petunia, four-o'clocks, evening primrose, and nicotiana, or flowering tobacco.

You must also include plants for the caterpillars. If you don't, you will attract only "passersby," and the adults will go elsewhere when it is time to lay eggs. Some common caterpillar host plants include cabbage and broccoli, carrot-family plants such as parsley and dill, and trees such as willow, hackberry, and sassafras. Your property might be large enough to have your own meadow. In any event you might experiment; if one plant doesn't seem to be attractive to local species, then try another.

Most importantly, avoid using pesticides on your garden! Butterflies like "weediness" anyway and will be encouraged by a few dandelions and clovers in the lawn.

Conservation

The effects of civilization have reduced the amount and variety of native habitats at least since the arrival of European colonists. While a few species have benefited from the intervention of humans — the Gypsy Moth, for example — many others have declined or disappeared. Several butterflies and moths, mostly western species, have already become extinct, and there are about 20 kinds of butterflies and moths on the U.S. Endangered Species List. Many states and provinces have lists of additional species that they consider to be endangered, threatened, or of special concern.

Conservationists ofien focus on saving endangered habitats rather than individual species. If the habitat is safe, all the species living there may survive. If the habitat disappears, the species will go with it. Some ecosystems that are especially threatened include the Florida Keys, the brushlands of the Lower Rio Grande Valley, the pine-oak barrens of the Northeast, the coastal dunes of California, and freshwater wetlands all over North America.

You can do your share by helping to conserve local habitats or by becoming active in local or national conservation organzations. The Xerces Society is one group dedicated to the conservation of invertebrates, including butterflies and moths.

Insect collecting is not usually a threat to butterfly or moth populations, but it is never wise to collect large numbers from small local populations or to trample the habitats of rare species.

How To Use This Book

All the butterflies and moths described in this book are shown in at least one color illustration. Sometimes we show both upperside and underside or, where the sexes are different, both male and female. We show the species in natural postures as much as possible. Often, though, an insect's markings would be hidden if it were not shown with its wings spread, as it would appear in a collection.

In the text, we describe each species' most obvious field marks. The insect's preferred habitats and its geographic range in North America are given. We also list the food plants of many of the adult insects and a few of the caterpillars.

The species in this book are identified by their common names. If you keep studying butterflies and moths, however, you will eventually want to learn their scientific names. The same butterfly may have different common names in various parts of the country, but scientific names are the same all over the world. Scientific names are given in the index.

To identify a species, observe it closely, noting its size, color, and most obvious markings. Then look through the plates for the butterfly or moth that is most similar. Check the habitat and geographic range given for that species. If all is in agreement, you have probably made a correct identification. Remember, this guide covers only the most common species, so your butterfly may be a close relative to the species described.

Butterflies

Swallowtails and Parnassians

This worldwide group is a favorite among butterfly enthusiasts because many of its members are large and brightly colored. Parnassians, with translucent white or yellow wings, are found only in the Northern Hemisphere. We have 3 species in the mountains of western North America. Most swallowtails, distinguished by their "tails," are tropical, but there are about 30 kinds in North America.

CLODIUS PARNASSIAN **2 – 2½ in.**

With its almost *transparent wings* and *circular red spots* on the hindwing, this midsummer butterfly is found in high mountains of the Pacific states and north into British Columbia. The butterflies fly near the ground in sunny areas. The caterpillars eat the leaves of bleeding-heart and, unlike most butterflies, there is a slight cocoon spun around its chrysalis.

PHOEBUS PARNASSIAN **1¾ – 2½ in.**

This is the most common parnassian; it is widespread in most western U.S. mountain ranges and north into western Canada as well. Its white wings are only *slightly translucent*, and there are black, gray, and *red markings* on *both wings*. Look for Phoebus Parnassian in sunny habitats.

PIPE-VINE SWALLOWTAIL **2¾ – 5⅛ in.**

The caterpillar of this species eats only leaves of pipe-vines. The adults fly with rapid wingbeats and continue to flutter their wings even when visiting flowers. Upper hindwings are *iridescent blue-green*, and there is a row of of *7 round, large, orange spots* on the hindwing below. Most common in the South; found in both eastern mountain forests and western desert flats. Adults are distasteful to birds and are models for mimics such as the Eastern Tiger Swallowtail and Red-spotted Purple, which look similar but are quite edible to birds.

CLODIUS
PARNASSIAN
male
female
PHOEBUS
PARNASSIAN
male
PIPE-VINE
SWALLOWTAIL
male

Kite Swallowtails

These swallowtails are distinguished by their exceptionally long tails. There are 140 species that are found principally in the American tropics. The Zebra Swallowtail is the only common kite swallowtail in North America.

ZEBRA SWALLOWTAIL **2½ – 4 in.**

With its *long tails* fluttering behind it like streamers, this *black-striped, greenish white* butterfly prefers flat forested areas near rivers or swamps. It is limited to the eastern half of the U.S. and is occasionally found in southern Ontario. Its caterpillars eat leaves of young pawpaw plants. Adults have short tongues but are fond of such flowers as water-willow, dogbane, and blackberry.

Fluted Swallowtails

North American species of this group feature yellow and black patterns. More than 200 species are found worldwide.

BLACK SWALLOWTAIL **3⅛ – 4½ in.**

This is the most widespread swallowtail, ranging from coast to coast and from the South to southern Canada. There are 4 other less common but similar swallowtails. Both sexes are mainly *black*, but males have a narrow *yellow band* on both wings. Females usually lack the yellow band but have an iridescent blue band on each hindwing. The butterflies fly in open areas, including vacant lots, neglected areas, and gardens. If you grow parsley, carrots, or dill, the odds are that you will find Black Swallowtail caterpillars in your garden. Nectar flowers include butterfly milkweed, thistles, and red clover.

ZEBRA
SWALLOWTAIL
BLACK SWALLOWTAIL
male
female

ANISE SWALLOWTAIL **3¼ – 3½ in.**

This is a western species that is similar to the Black Swallowtail but has a *broad yellow forewing band* and a mainly yellow hindwing. The butterfly has adapted to cities and suburbs in California and Oregon, where caterpillars eat fennel (also called anise). Males fly to hilltops and establish perches where they wait for females with whom they court. You can find these butterflies nectaring at flowers such as red valerian and yellow star thistle.

SCHAUS' SWALLOWTAIL **3⅝ – 4⅝ in.**

This is an *endangered* species. Schaus' Swallowtail is found on only a few islands in the Upper Florida Keys. Development, hurricanes, and pesticides intended for mosquitoes greatly reduced the numbers of this rare swallowtail, but conservation efforts have brought it back from the brink of extinction.

GIANT SWALLOWTAIL **4 – 6¼ in.**

This large swallowtail is distinguished by the *diagonal yellow spot band* on each forewing. The Giant Swallowtail is our largest butterfly, although occasional Eastern Tiger Swallowtail females are a bit larger. The Giant Swallowtail lives in the Southeast and other southern states, where its caterpillars, sometimes called Orange Dogs or Orange Puppies, can be a nuisance in orange groves. The caterpillars also eat leaves of prickly ash, hop tree, Hercules-club, and torchwood. Look for it on rocky hillsides and in pine woods, citrus groves, and gardens. The butterflies nectar at many flowers, including lantana, thistle, and boneset. The adults keep breeding and flying year-round in Florida and south Texas.

ANISE
SWALLOWTAIL
SCHAUS'
SWALLOWTAIL
GIANT
SWALLOWTAIL

EASTERN TIGER SWALLOWTAIL **3⅝ – 6½ in.**

Except for the Monarch, the Tiger Swallowtails are North America's most familiar butterflies. The Eastern Tiger is well named for its vertical *black stripes* on *yellow wings*. There are 2 female forms — one is yellow and black, like the male, and the second has all-black wings. The black female is most prevalent in the South and is believed to mimic the Pipe-vine Swallowtail. The Eastern Tiger Swallowtail is found in the eastern U.S. and is replaced in the northernmost states and southern Canada by the smaller Canadian Tiger Swallowtail. Look for this butterfly in woodlands, suburban gardens, and parks. The adults have several flights from spring through late summer. The swallowtails nectar at flowers such as lilac, buttonbush, thistles, and milkweeds. Caterpillars live in folded leaf shelters and eat the leaves of yellow poplar, wild cherry, and sweetbay.

WESTERN TIGER SWALLOWTAIL **2¾ – 4 in.**

This butterfly replaces the Eastern Tiger Swallowtail in the western U.S. and southwestern Canada. It has *narrower wings* than the Eastern Tiger and *lacks orange* on the underside. Look for it in early summer. The Western Tiger is found in a variety of habitats, including wooded suburbs and woodlands near streams and rivers. You can find adult butterflies nectaring at flowers such as lilac, buckeye, yerba santa, thistles, zinnia, and abelia. The caterpillars eat leaves of cottonwood, willow, aspen, wild cherry, and ash.

black form
EASTERN TIGER
SWALLOWTAIL
yellow form
WESTERN TIGER
SWALLOWTAIL

SPICEBUSH SWALLOWTAIL **3⅝ – 4⅞ in.**

Identify the adults by their *spoon-shaped tails* and by their bright *green* (male) or *iridescent blue* (female) hindwings. You must seek these primarily black swallowtails in deciduous woods or woody swamps, where they can be found flying low and fast through shaded areas. The Spicebush Swallowtail is found only in the eastern U.S. and extreme southern Ontario. The caterpillars live in folded leaf shelters and eat the leaves of sassafras or spicebush. Both sexes are thought to be edible mimics of the distasteful Pipe-vine Swallowtail.

PALAMEDES SWALLOWTAIL **4½ – 5⅛ in.**

This large, brown-black swallowtail has a *yellow band* above and *yellow-filled tails* on its hindwings. You can find this attractive butterfly in swampy forests and other moist habitats on the south Atlantic and Gulf coastal plains. You may see the Palamedes Swallowtail from spring to fall; look for them on thistles, a favorite nectar plant. The caterpillars eat the leaves of red bay and may occasionally dine on sassafras.

female
SPICEBUSH
SWALLOWTAIL
male
PALAMEDES
SWALLOWTAIL

Whites and Sulphurs

The members of this large family are primarily medium-sized, white or yellow butterflies that tend to fly in open, sunny areas.

Whites

The whites include a number of common species, most of which eat the leaves, flowers, or seed pods of mustard family plants.

PINE WHITE **2 – 2¾ in.**

This predominantly western butterfly is identified by the *black bar* on the front edge of the forewing and the *black lining* on the hindwing veins below. It is usually found in pine forests. Occasionally, the butterflies are so common that pine forests are stripped of needles by the caterpillars.

CHECKERED WHITE **1¾ – 2½ in.**

This very common white can be distinguished by its *black, checkered pattern.* It is found throughout the contiguous U.S. and southernmost Canada. Seek it in open areas, such as vacant lots, roadsides, or desert plains. The Checkered White's caterpillars feed on the seed pods and flowers of plants in the mustard family.

MUSTARD WHITE **1⅜ – 2¼ in.**

This butterfly is called the Veined White in the Far West. The butterflies may be *immaculate white* above and below or may have 1 or 2 *faint black forewing spots* and *gray-green* or *yellow-green veins* on the hindwings below. It ranges from the Northeast and mountainous West north to Alaska and northern Canada. Look for it in damp woodlands and adjacent edges.

CABBAGE BUTTERFLY **1¾ – 2¼ in.**

This may be our most common butterfly, found in yards and gardens throughout most of the U.S. and southern Canada. The butterfly has a *black forewing tip* and the hindwing underside is *yellow-green* or *gray-green.* The green caterpillars can be a pest on cabbages, broccoli, and kale.

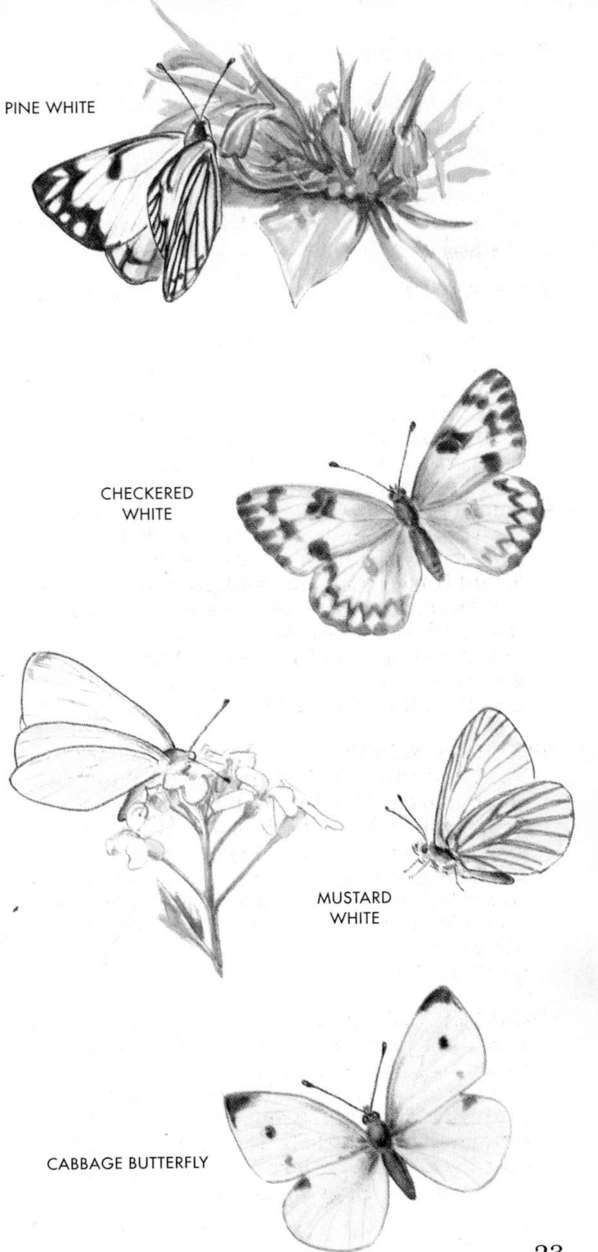
PINE WHITE
CHECKERED WHITE
MUSTARD WHITE
CABBAGE BUTTERFLY

GREAT SOUTHERN WHITE **2½–3½ in.**

This butterfly is primarily a denizen of our southern coasts. The male can be told by the *zigzag black* forewing margin. The female may be either of 2 forms — one gray and the other cloudy black. Both female forms have a *small black spot* near the front edge of the forewing. The butterflies can be found most of the year in coastal marshes, dunes, and nearby open fields. The Great Southern White occasionally migrates along the coastline and may stray inland. The caterpillars eat the leaves of a variety of cabbage family plants.

LARGE MARBLE **1½–2 in.**

Distinguish this butterfly by the *green marbling* on the underside of its hindwings. The Large Marble is widespread in the western mountains, where it can be found in meadows or along streams. There are 3 other marbles in North America. Only one generation of adults flies each year, emerging from their chrysalids as early as February or as late as July. The caterpillars eat the buds and flowers of mustards and rock cresses.

FALCATE ORANGE TIP **1½–1¾ in.**

This is one of the earliest spring butterflies in the eastern United States. It can be identified by its *pointed wingtips* and dense *dark green marbling* below. Only males have the orange wingtips. Look for it in spring in moist woods or by streams. The green caterpillars eat the flowers and seed pods of several mustard plants.

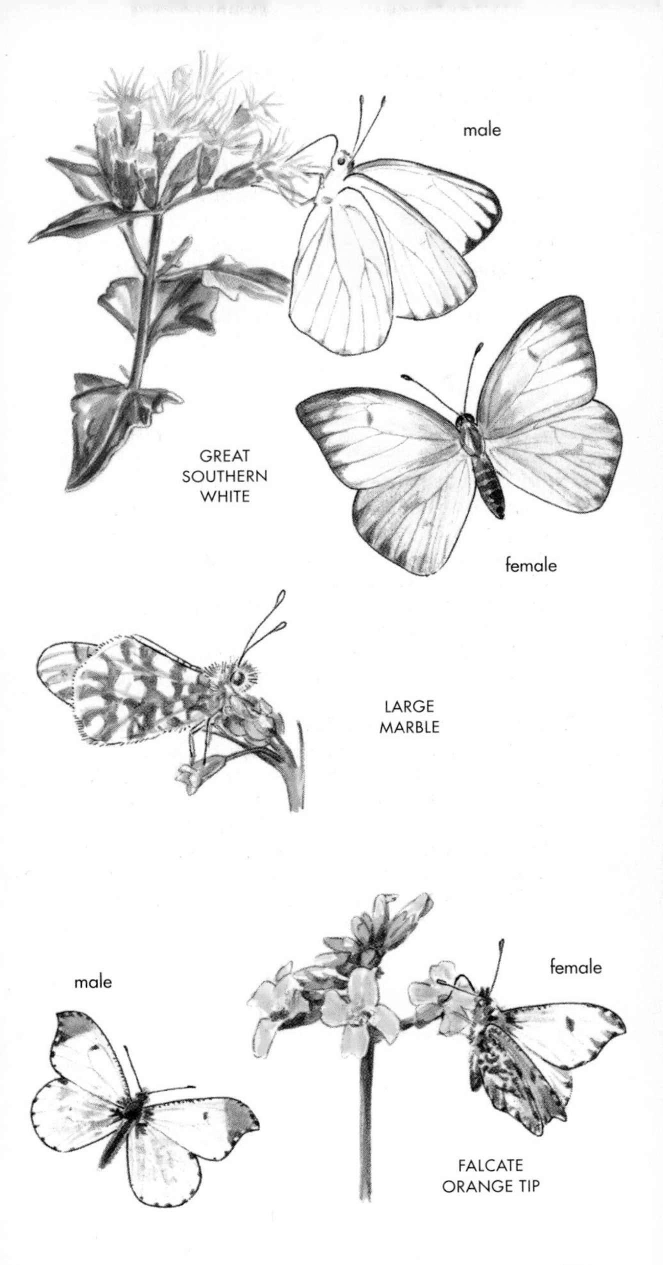
male
GREAT
SOUTHERN
WHITE
female
LARGE
MARBLE
male
female
FALCATE
ORANGE TIP

SARA ORANGE TIP **$1^3/_8 - 1^7/_8$ in.**

The tips of this white's forewings are *rounded*, and each has a *large orange patch* — the patch is smaller on females. Underside of hindwing has highly fractured *dark green* or *yellow-green marbling*. The Sara Orange Tip is usually found along streams or canyon bottoms, but you might find egg-laying females along hillsides or ridge tops. This variable butterfly is found in mountains, deserts, and coastal hills throughout much of western North America. The caterpillars eat the flowers and seed pods of many plants in the mustard family

Sulphurs

Most sulphurs are small to medium-sized yellow or orange butterflies that are abundant in open, sunny areas. Most species have both yellow and white female forms. The caterpillars eat the leaves, flowers, or seed pods of legumes and a few other plant families.

CLOUDED SULPHUR **$2 - 2^3/_4$ in.**

This common butterfly is *clear yellow* with *black outer margins* on both wings. There are both clear yellow and white female forms. The white female form is virtually identical to that of the Alfalfa Butterfly (see page 28). You can find Clouded Sulphurs in fields or roadsides almost everywhere in North America, from spring to the fall. The white-striped green caterpillars eat leaves of clovers, sweet clover, and alfalfa.

female
SARA
ORANGE TIP
male
female
male
CLOUDED
SULPHUR

ALFALFA BUTTERFLY **2 – 2¾ in.**

Any common sulphur with at least some *orange* is probably this species. In the South, however, be careful to separate it from the Sleepy Orange (see page 30). There are both orange and white female forms of the Alfalfa Butterfly. This butterfly is most common in the South and West, but it may be found through much of North America. Like the Clouded Sulphur, it is found in a variety of open habitats. Its caterpillars are found mainly on alfalfa, but they can eat the leaves of many clovers and other legumes as well. There are several kinds of similar sulphurs in the West and North with which the above two species might be confused, but they are rarer and found in only a few areas.

DOG FACE **2¼ – 3 in.**

A *poodle head* outline on the *pointed forewing* distinguishes this large yellow butterfly, although the female's dog face is faint. This is a tropical butterfly that resides in our southern states. Occasionally, it wanders north to form temporary populations. It is found in open, scrubby fields and the edges of woodlands. Its caterpillars eat the leaves of legumes such as wild indigo, leadplant, and prairie clovers. Its close relative, the California Dog Face, is the official state insect of California.

male
ALFALFA
BUTTERFLY
female
yellow
form
female
female
white form
male
DOG FACE

CLOUDLESS SULPHUR **2½ – 3 in.**

This large *all-yellow*, high-flying butterfly is unmistakable. The Cloudless Sulphur resides in subtropical areas of the South but can colonize more northern areas in the summer. You may see the butterflies in a wide range of open, sunny habitats. The Cloudless Sulphur spends the winter as an adult. The butterflies occasionally migrate, especially in late summer or fall. Favored flowers for nectaring include lantana, bougainvillea, turk's-cap, and hibiscus. The caterpillars eat the leaves of senna, cassias, and partridge pea.

LITTLE SULPHUR **1¼ – 1¾ in.**

This is a *small, all-yellow* butterfly with *black borders* and a *small black spot* on the forewing. You will find this butterfly most often in scrubby areas or in small, sunny openings in woods. It is most common in the Southeast but may wander to more northern states. Winter is passed in the adult stage, and there are several summer flights. The adults nectar at the flowers of a variety of small, low-growing plants.

SLEEPY ORANGE **1½ – 2¼ in.**

When in flight this butterfly is anything but "sleepy." Its wings are *pure orange* with broad *irregular black margins*. The butterflies can be seen flying or nectaring in open fields, desert foothills, or open woods. The Sleepy Orange is a southern species, but some may fly to more northern states and very rarely to southern Canada. The adults overwinter in wooded areas. Caterpillars eat the leaves of cassias, including partridge pea.

CLOUDLESS
SULPHUR
female
male
LITTLE
SULPHUR
female
SLEEPY
ORANGE
male

DAINTY SULPHUR **1 – 1¼ in.**

This is a *tiny, yellow* butterfly that has *black wingtips* and a *black bar* on the trailing edge of the forewing. Watch for it flying within a few inches of the ground along roadsides and dry, open places. This southern butterfly regularly flies to more northern areas in summer.

Gossamer Wings

This family includes harvesters, coppers, hairstreaks, and blues. Many of these butterflies rub their hindwings together when alighted; this may be a way to draw the attention of predators away from the body.

HARVESTER **1⅛ – 1¼ in.**

This unique butterfly is *orange and black* above, while below the hindwings are orange-brown with *faint white scrawls*. The Harvester is an eastern species, usually found in sunny openings along small streams or in wooded swamps. The carnivorous caterpillars eat woolly aphids.

Coppers

Coppers are named for their iridescent purple, red, or bronze colors. They usually perch with open wings and are rapid fliers. These species live in western mountains.

TAILED COPPER **1⅛ – 1⅜ in.**

The undersides of this *tailed* copper have a *gray and white* scrawly pattern. Males are shiny purple above, females have an orange and black checkered pattern. Usually found in streams, canyons, or shady hillsides in a wide variety of habitats ranging from oak woodlands to sagebrush-juniper scrub.

AMERICAN COPPER **1 – 1⅜ in.**

The *iridescent, fiery red-orange forewing* is distinctive. There is also a *red-orange line* along the outer margin of the hindwing below. In the East, this butterfly is found in open weedy fields and along roadsides. In the Arctic and some western mountains the American Copper is found on rocky slopes.

DAINTY SULPHUR

HARVESTER

at rest

male

female

TAILED COPPER

AMERICAN COPPER

at rest

BRONZE COPPER **1⅛ – 1⅜ in.**

When perched, the *chalk-white, black-dotted* hindwing undersides have a *broad red-orange border.* Males are purplish brown above, whereas females are checkered orange and black. Look for Bronze Coppers in wet areas along streams or in marshes. The butterflies range from the Northeast, including southern Canada, west to the Midwest, southern prairie provinces, and Rocky Mountains. Look for them in summer and fall. The caterpillars eat the young leaves of water dock and curled dock.

BLUE COPPER **1⅛ – 1⅜ in.**

Unlike any other copper, the male is *iridescent sky blue* above, while the female is usually gray or gray-brown with a small amount of blue. The butterflies are usually found on open, rocky slopes in mountains, foothills, or sagebrush scrub. You can find the butterfly in summer, in many of the mountain ranges of the western U.S. and extreme southwestern Canada. Adults nectar at flowers of wild buckwheat, Indian hemp, and composites. The caterpillars eat the leaves of wild buckwheats.

PURPLISH COPPER **1⅛ – 1½ in.**

Both sexes have a *zigzag orange border* on their hindwings. Males are iridescent purplish brown, while females are checkered orange and dark brown. The butterfly is a close relative of the more northern Dorcas Copper. You can find the Purplish Copper most often in marshes or mountain meadows. It is found from the upper Midwest and southern Canada westward to the Pacific Coast. Adults nectar at a wide variety of flowers including mints, asters, and rabbitbrush. The caterpillars eat the leaves of various docks and knotweeds.

male
female
BRONZE
COPPER
male
female
BLUE
COPPER
male
female
PURPLISH COPPER

Hairstreaks

Hairstreaks are named for the short, thread-like tails found on the hindwings of most species. Many hairstreaks are brown and are found in or near woodlands, but some of our species are iridescent blue or purple above, and others are bright green below. The adults perch with closed wings and fly rapidly.

GREAT PURPLE HAIRSTREAK **1¼ – 2 in.**

Both sexes are *iridescent blue* (not purple!) above and *black* below. There are 2 long tails at the trailing edge of each hindwing. This butterfly may be found in a wide range of habitats, including desert hills, swampy forests, and mountain canyons. The Great Purple Hairstreak is found in the southern half of the U.S. and ranges south into the tropics. You can find it from spring through the fall, nectaring on flowers such as mint, Hercules-club, mesquite, and shepherd's needle. The caterpillars feed only on the leaves of mistletoe.

COLORADO HAIRSTREAK **1¼ – 1½ in.**

You can find this spectacular *purple* butterfly perched on its caterpillar host plant, Gambel's Oak, during July and early August. The Colorado Hairstreak is found in oak woods or oak-pine forest in the southern Rock Mountains and in Southwestern mountains. The adults occasionally nectar at yellow flowers in the composite family.

FLORIDA ATALA **1⅝ – 2 in.**

In subtropical southern Florida, you may locate the Atala sitting on its caterpillar host, a plant called coontie, a cycad. The *black* butterfly has a *red abdomen* and rows of iridescent *blue spots* on the hindwings below. Look for this tropical butterfly in hardwood hammocks or parks in the southern tip of Florida. The Atala may be found all year but is most common in early summer.

GREAT
PURPLE
HAIRSTREAK
female
male
female
male
COLORADO
HAIRSTREAK
male
female
FLORIDA
ATALA

CORAL HAIRSTREAK **1 – 1½ in.**

This brown hairstreak *lacks tails* and has a row of *coral red spots* on the outer edge of each hindwing below. It occurs in many habitats including city parks, foothill canyons, and woodland edges over most of the northern half of the U.S. and southern Canada. Adults nectar at milkweeds, dogbane, wild buckwheat, and rabbitbrush.

CALIFORNIA HAIRSTREAK **1 – 1¼ in.**

This is a brown butterfly with some *orange on the outer edge* of the forewing, and a row of *round black spots on the underside.* You may find the California Hairstreak in several habitats in different parts of its range; these include foothill canyons, sagebrush-juniper scrub, and oak woodland. Its range includes much of the western U.S. and portions of extreme southwestern Canada. Adults may be found nectaring at a variety of plants including Indian hemp, wild buckwheat, white sweet clover, buckeye, and yerba santa.

BANDED HAIRSTREAK **1¼ – 1½ in.**

This common eastern brown hairstreak has a *band of dark dashes* on the underside of each hindwing. The butterfly is usually found in or near woodlands, especially those with oaks or hickories. It is found in most of the eastern U.S. and southern Canada, but has a population in the foothills of the southern Rocky Mountains. Adults nectar at many flowers including common milkweed, chinquapin, New Jersey tea, white sweet clover, and dogbane.

SHERIDAN'S HAIRSTREAK **⅞ – 1⅛ in.**

This small spring butterfly is *mouse gray* above. Below, its hindwings are *apple green* with a bold *white central line.* You can find these sprites from low western foothill canyons to near timberline in much of the western U.S. Depending on the elevation where they live, the adults may fly in spring or summer.

CORAL
HAIRSTREAK

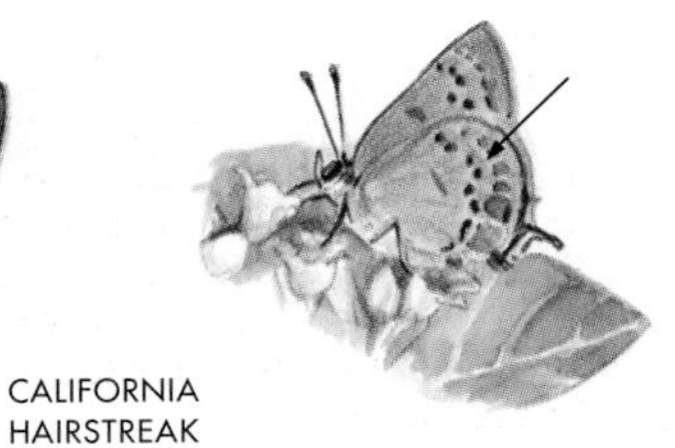

CALIFORNIA
HAIRSTREAK

BANDED
HAIRSTREAK

SHERIDAN'S HAIRSTREAK

OLIVE HAIRSTREAK **1 – 1¼ in.**

If you tap junipers or eastern redcedars with a stick or net handle, one or more of these small hairstreaks with *yellow-green* hindwing undersides marked with *white lines* may fly up and then flutter down to alight again. The butterflies are found in old fields, rocky bluffs, or foothill canyons in most of the U.S. and southern Canada. The adults take nectar at a variety of flowers including mustards, composites, wild buckwheat, and dogbane.

BROWN ELFIN **⅞ – 1⅛ in.**

This well-named butterfly is a study in brown. The hindwings are *red-brown* with an *irregular dark line.* Brown Elfins can be found in several habitats including barrens, oak-pine woodlands, and foothill canyons. It ranges through most of North America, especially the northern states, mountainous areas, and southern Canada. Look for the adults at flowers or at rest on heaths and buckthorns, their caterpillar host plants.

EASTERN PINE ELFIN **1⅛ – 1¼ in.**

This butterfly is distinguished by the underside of the hindwings, which are *red-brown with darker checks* and scalloped markings. The butterflies can be located in barrens, near pine woods, or in openings along wood edges. Look for them through much of eastern North America during spring. The adults nectar at flowers such as daisy fleabane, New Jersey tea, and wild plum.

RED-BANDED HAIRSTREAK **⅞ – 1¼ in.**

These small hairstreaks are dusky black and blue above and have a *red-orange band* on the hindwing below. They are common along wood edges or scrubby fields in the Southeast. A related butterfly ranges from central Texas south into the tropics. The adults nectar at dogbane, sumac, sweet pepperbush, and shepherd's needle.

OLIVE HAIRSTREAK

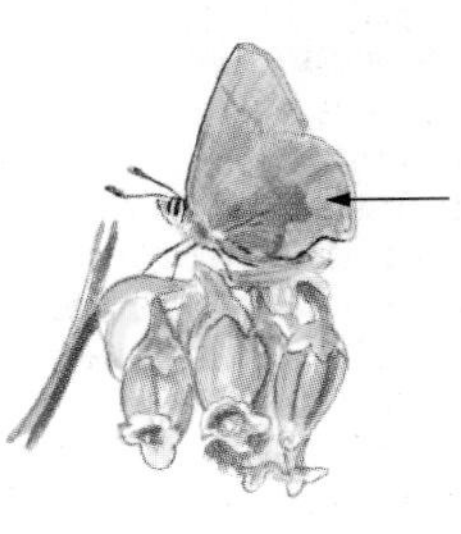

BROWN ELFIN

EASTERN PINE ELFIN

RED-BANDED HAIRSTREAK

WHITE-M HAIRSTREAK **1¼– 1⅝ in.**

The adults are *iridescent blue* above and gray below with a median *white stripe* that forms an *M* near the hindwing's trailing edge. These butterflies are usually found near oak woods but may be found in such places as marshes and fields. They are most common in the Southeast. Adults nectar at flowers such as viburnum, common milkweed, and sweet pepperbush.

GRAY HAIRSTREAK **1⅛– 1⅜ in.**

This is the most common, most widespread hairstreak in North America. It is distinguished by its *gray* color and *orange spot* at the trailing edge of the hindwing. It can be found in almost any habitat. Males may be seen on hilltops in late afternoon. Adults nectar on many plants with small flowers.

Blues

On the upperside, males of most blues are iridescent blue and females are brown. Underneath, blues are gray with small black spots or stripes. Most species are small to tiny. The West has most species, but 2 species are common in most of the East.

PYGMY BLUE **⅝– ¾ in.**

This is the *smallest* butterfly in North America. The adults are *red-brown* above and gray with tiny black spots below. Look for them in desert flats, tidal areas, along railroad tracks, or in other waste places. The butterflies are most common in the Southwest, but regularly invade more northern areas in summer. The similar Eastern Pygmy Blue is found in coastal areas in the Southeast.

MARINE BLUE **1 – 1⅛ in.**

You can identify this butterfly by the *violet blue* color above and the *fine barring* on the underside of both wings. In much of the Southwest look for these butterflies in suburban gardens and in desert scrub. Adults nectar at many plants including mesquite, sweet clover, and mints.

WHITE-M
HAIRSTREAK
GRAY
HAIRSTREAK
PYGMY BLUE
MARINE
BLUE
male
female

EASTERN TAILED BLUE ¾ – 1⅛ in.

This species is most common in eastern North America but is found from coast to coast and ranges south into the tropics. You can easily identify it, since it and its close relative the Western Tailed Blue are the only blue species with a fine *hairlike tail* on the trailing edge of each hindwing. There is a small *orange mark* near the base of each tail. Males are blue above, and females are mainly brown. The butterflies are found in many open, sunny areas with low-growing vegetation, including fields, meadows, and overgrown lawns. Adults nectar at flowers such as white sweet clover, dogbane, butterfly milkweed, and daisy fleabane.

SPRING AZURE 1⅛ – 1¼ in.

This is a widespread, famliar blue that can be identified by its *powdery blue* color and *lightly marked gray-white* undersides. There are no orange marks. Females are darker than males. This species is found in a variety of woodland and scrub habitats from coast to coast and from the subarctic south into the tropics. They usually fly in spring and early summer, but they may rarely be found in late summer. Adult males visit wet mud or sand and nectar at a variety of plants that often serve as caterpillar host plants. These include dogwoods, New Jersey tea, buckeye, and viburnum.

SILVERY BLUE ⅞ – 1¼ in.

This butterfly can be identified by the *silvery blue* of the males and the row of *uniformly round black spots* on the undersides. The Palos Verdes Blue is an *endangered* subspecies that was found near Los Angeles. Its last habitat was destroyed by development. Look for the Silvery Blue near streams, moist meadows, or open hillsides. It is found in northern areas from coast to coast, but is most common in western mountains and the subarctic. Adults emerge from February to early July, depending on latitude and elevation.

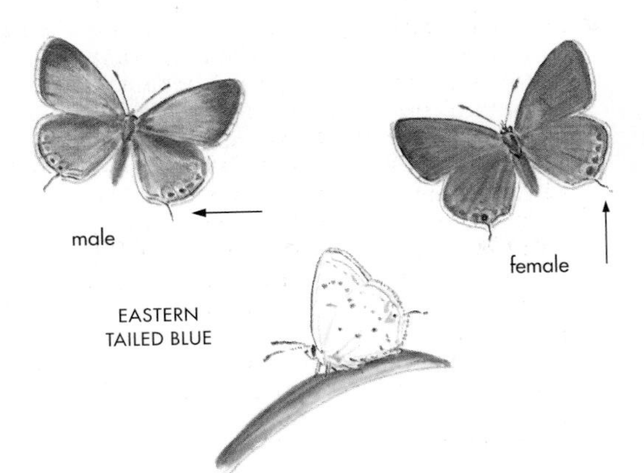

female

male

SPRING AZURE

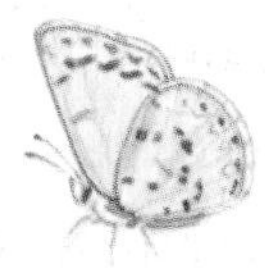

male

SILVERY
BLUE

MELISSA BLUE **1 – 1⅜ in.**

The species has a *row of orange marginal marks* on the undersides of both wings. Males are blue above, and females are brown and blue with orange margins. Melissa Blue occurs in open areas such as waste areas, foothills, and meadows, and it ranges from coast to coast in the northern U.S. and southern Canada.

The Karner Blue is an *endangered* eastern subspecies of Melissa Blue that lives only in pine barrens, a disappearing habitat. In the East, the caterpillars of the Karner Blue only eat the young leaves of lupine, while in the West they feed upon a wide variety of legumes.

ACMON BLUE **1 – 1⅛ in.**

Identify this butterfly by the *orange band* on each hindwing above and below. Males are blue above and females are brown. The Acmon Blue is found in open, dry habitats and waste areas in the Great Plains, the West, and southern Canada. Adults nectar at a variety of flowers including wild buckwheats, alfalfa, and composites. Caterpillars eat the leaves and flowers of wild buckwheat and a variety of legumes.

BOISDUVAL'S BLUE **1⅛ – 1⅜ in.**

You can identify this variable species by its *dull blue* color, and the row of irregular black and white marks on the wings below. Look for the butterfly on open hillsides and meadows in mountainous areas of the western U.S. and southwestern Canada. Boisduval's Blues fly in late spring or summer. Caterpillars eat the young leaves of various lupine species.

The Mission Blue is an *endangered* subspecies of Boisduval's Blue that is found near San Francisco.

female

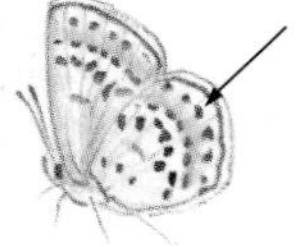

male

MELISSA
BLUE

male

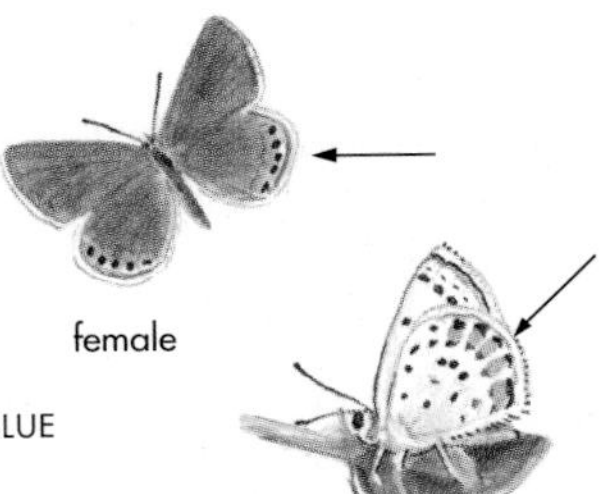

female

ACMON BLUE

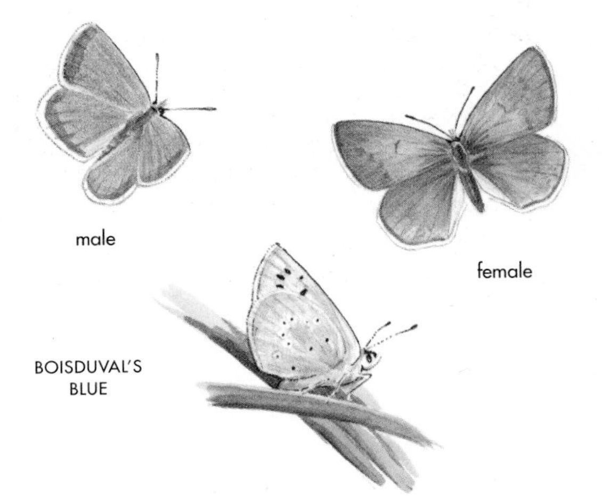

male

female

BOISDUVAL'S
BLUE

Metalmarks

Metalmarks are a tropical group with just a few species in North America. They perch with open wings, often on their host plants.

NORTHERN METALMARK **1⅛ – 1¼ in.**

Identify the Northern Metalmark by its *red-brown* color and *thin silver metallic lines.* You can find the butterflies in barrens or streamsides in the East. Adults nectar at ragwort and butterfly milkweed.

MORMON METALMARK **⅞ – 1¼ in.**

Identify these small butterflies by their *orange, black, and white checks* above and their gray or brownish flecked undersides. The Lange's Metalmark is an *endangered* subspecies found in central California. Look for the butterflies in desert hills, dry hillsides, or sand dunes. The butterflies are found on the Pacific coast and in the Southwest. The adults nectar on wild buckwheats and yellow composites.

Brushfoots

Almost all butterflies in the brushfoot family have very small front legs that are used not for walking but often for "tasting" plants. Many brushfoots do not visit flowers, feeding instead on animal droppings, sap flows, or decaying fruit.

AMERICAN SNOUT **1⅝ – 2 in.**

The American Snout has *long palps* that look like a long nose or snout. The forewing tips are *squared off.* The butterfly looks like a *dead leaf* when perched on a twig with its wings closed. American Snouts sometimes occur in incredible abundance and engage in mass migrations. At such times, you can find these butterflies in desert scrub or many kinds of woodland habitats. The butterflies are most common in the Southwest, but are resident generally in the South and may appear in the Midwest and southern New England. Adults nectar at many flowers including dogbane, sweet pepperbush, mesquite, and composites.

NORTHERN
METALMARK

MORMON
METALMARK

AMERICAN
SNOUT

GULF FRITILLARY **2½ – 3¾ in.**

You can identify this butterfly by its bright *red-orange* uppersides and the *long metallic silver marks* below. It flies with very shallow wingbeats. The butterflies are found in parks, suburban gardens, and the edges of tropical woods or hammocks. It is found across the southern portion of the U.S. but establishes temporary breeding colonies farther north. The butterflies are present all year in their areas of residence. Adults nectar at a variety of plants including lantana, shepherd's needle, and other composites.

ZEBRA **2¾ – 4 in.**

The Zebra is easily identified by its long *black wings* with thin *yellow stripes.* It usually flies very slowly, with shallow wingbeats. Zebras belong to a tropical group that has the unusual habit of collecting and feeding on pollen from flowers. Its preferred habitat is the understory of dense tropical or subtropical woodlands and hammocks. This butterfly is resident in southern Florida and south Texas, and occasionally appears in southeastern Arizona and elsewhere north of its normal range. The butterflies are found year round in their permanent habitats. You can find adults nectaring and collecting pollen at lantana and composites such as shepherd's needle.

VARIEGATED FRITILLARY **1¾ – 3⅛ in.**

This is an orange fritillary with *angled wing margins* that *lacks silver marks* below. It flies with shallow wingbeats. Variegated Fritillaries may be found in a wide variety of open habitats including roadsides, desert scrub, and foothill meadows. It is resident across the southern U.S. but regularly ranges north and breeds throughout most of the U.S. and southern Canada. Variegated Fritillaries can be seen most of the year in the South. The adults nectar at a wide variety of flowers.

GULF
FRITILLARY
ZEBRA
VARIEGATED
FRITILLARY

REGAL FRITILLARY **3⅛ – 4⅛ in.**

This is a declining species that should be conserved wherever it is found. The Regal Fritillary can be identified by its *large size, red-orange* forewings with black spots, and the *black white-spotted* hindwings. Look for the Regal Fritillary in moist meadows and native prairies. Formerly, it ranged from the East through the Midwest to the Great Plains. Now it has disappeared from most of its former habitats and is common in only a few places west of the Mississippi. The adults fly from mid-June until mid-August. They can be found nectaring at milkweeds and thistles. Caterpillars eat the leaves of birdfoot violet and probably other violets as well.

DIANA **3½ – 4½ in.**

The Diana is a large, magnificent butterfly. The *orange* males have *black outer margins* and the females are *iridescent blue* or *blue-green* above and black below. The Diana once had a wider range, but now it is found only in or near rich bottomland woodlands in the Appalachians and sparingly in the Ozarks. Look for Dianas in July and August. Adults nectar at milkweeds. Females wait until midafternoon to arrive at patches of nectar plants. Caterpillars eat the leaves of violets.

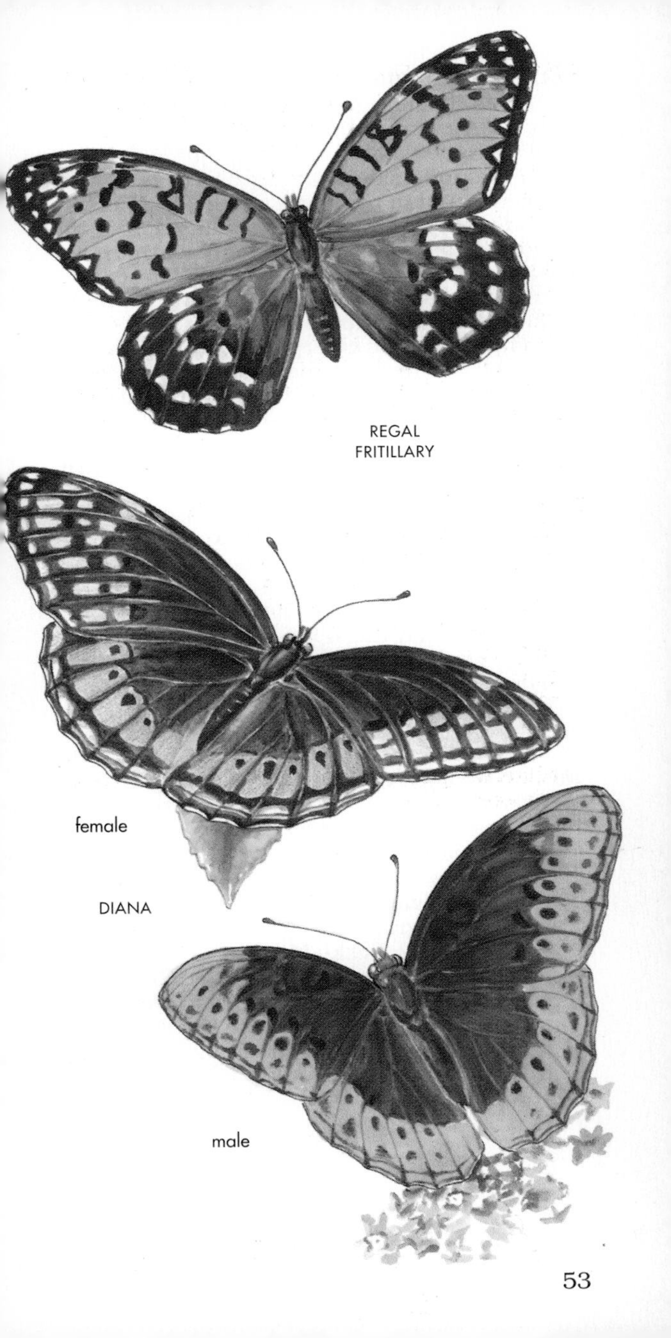
REGAL
FRITILLARY
female
DIANA
male

GREAT SPANGLED FRITILLARY 3 – 4 in.

This is the most familiar eastern fritillary. It is a large orange butterfly with prominent silver spots and a *broad buff marginal band* on the underside of the hindwing. It is most often found in meadows and fields. You can find the Great Spangled Fritillary across the northern and central U.S. and southern Canada. The adults fly from mid-June to mid-August. They nectar on many plants including milkweeds, thistles, and other composites. The caterpillars eat the leaves of violets. There are many species and geographic varieties of silverspots and fritillaries, especially in the West.

SILVER-BORDERED FRITILLARY 1⅝ – 2⅛ in.

This is the most widespread "lesser fritillary." It has an extensive network of *metallic silver spots* on the underside of the hindwings. Look for this small orange butterfly in wet meadows, bogs, and fields. It ranges across the northern U.S. and is found throughout much of Canada and Alaska. The adults nectar on yellow composites, bush cinquefoil, and other plants. The caterpillars eat the leaves of violets.

MEADOW FRITILLARY 1⅝ – 2 in.

This common small orange fritillary has a *squared-off forewing tip* and a mottled *purple-brown* hindwing underside. Look for it in open fields, meadows, and roadsides. It is common in much of the eastern U.S. and north to central Canada. It also ranges south into the Rocky Mountains. Meadow Fritillaries are frequent visitors to flowers of yellow composites such as black-eyed susans. The caterpillars eat the leaves of violets. There are several other similar lesser fritillaries in the West and to the north.

GREAT
SPANGLED
FRITILLARY
SILVER-BORDERED
FRITILLARY
MEADOW
FRITILLARY

BORDERED PATCH **1⅜ – 1⅞ in.**

This is a medium-sized *black* butterfly with an *orange band* on the hindwing. The Bordered Patch varies considerably depending on location. Two forms are shown here. It is found in scrubby fields and desert scrub over much of the Southwest. You can find adults through most of the year. Look for it nectaring on composite flowers. Caterpillars feed in groups on the leaves of sunflowers and other composites.

SILVERY CHECKERSPOT **1⅝ – 2 in.**

This medium orange butterfly can be identified by the marginal row of *white-centered hindwing spots*. Look for the Silvery Checkerspot in woodland openings or meadows near or adjacent to streams. This species is found in the eastern U.S., Southwest, and southern Canada. Adults nectar at a variety of flowers including dogbane, milkweeds, and yellow composites. The caterpillars feed in small groups on the leaves of several kinds of composites.

NORTHERN CHECKERSPOT **1⅜ – 1⅞ in.**

This small *red-orange* checkerspot can be told by the checkered pattern of *flat white and orange spots* on the underside of the hindwing. Along the Pacific Coast, females may be black above. It is found along streams and on moist slopes in the mountains and foothills of the western U.S. and southern Canada. Males perch and patrol along streambeds in their search for females with whom to mate. Look for adults nectaring in spring or early summer at yellow composites. The caterpillars eat the leaves of asters and other composites. There are several other very similar checkerspots in the West.

BORDERED
PATCH
dark form
SILVERY
CHECKERSPOT
NORTHERN CHECKERSPOT

FULVIA CHECKERSPOT **1⅜ – 2 in.**

Identify this small Southwestern butterfly by the hindwing underside, which is *cream* with *black-lined veins* and a black band enclosing *cream spots.* You can find this butterfly in arid hills and bluffs. Adult males have perches along ridges or hilltops. Adults nectar at small yellow composites. Caterpillars feed on Indian paintbrush.

PEARL CRESCENT **1¼ – 1⅝ in.**

You can identify this small orange butterfly by its *black borders* above and by the *tan hindwing* below with its *dark brown marginal patch.* There are several similar species, but this is by far the most abundant. It is found throughout most of the U.S. and southern Canada. Pearl Crescents fly from spring to fall. Adults nectar at a variety of small flowers. The eggs are laid in masses, and the caterpillars feed on the leaves of asters.

FIELD CRESCENT **1⅜ – 1¾ in.**

Identify this small crescent by its *black, yellow-spotted* uppersides and its *yellow-brown hindwing* underside. The butterfly is found from spring to fall in fields, meadows, and open hillsides. You can find the Field Crescent throughout most of the mountains of the western U.S. and Canada. Males patrol in search of mates. Caterpillars feed on leaves of asters.

MYLITTA CRESCENT **1⅛ – 1½ in.**

This is a small, *bright, pale orange* crescent with *narrow black marks.* It is found in weedy fields and along small streams in the foothills and lowlands of the western U.S. and southwestern Canada. You can find adults nectaring at the flowers of a variety of low plants. Caterpillars feed in groups on the leaves of thistles.

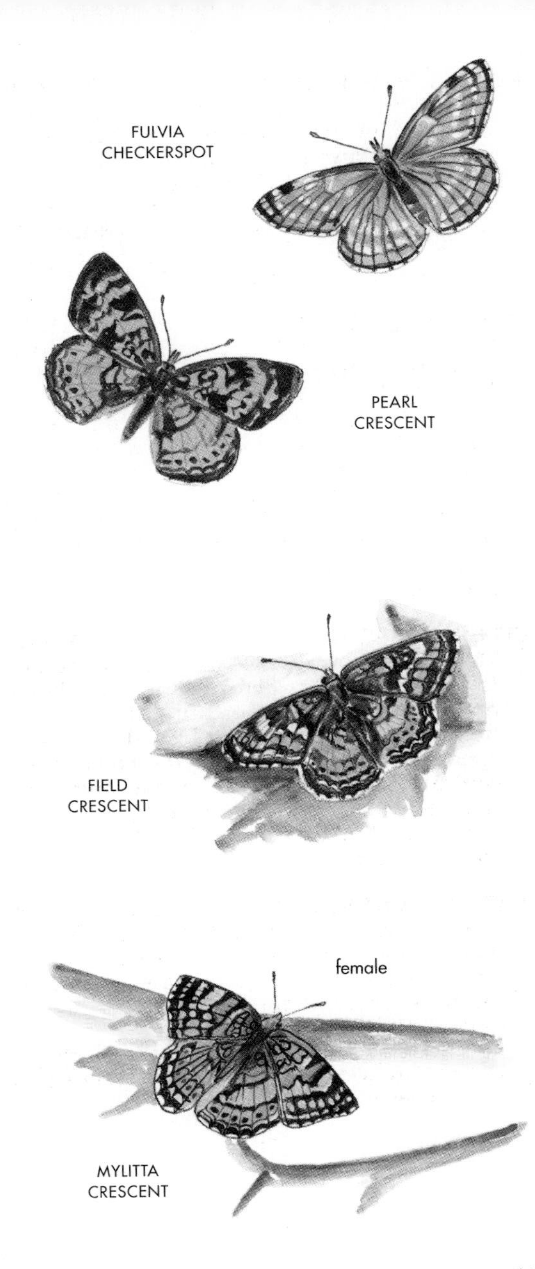
FULVIA
CHECKERSPOT
PEARL
CRESCENT
FIELD
CRESCENT
female
MYLITTA
CRESCENT

BALTIMORE **$1\frac{3}{4}$ – $2\frac{3}{4}$ in.**

This is the official state insect of Maryland. Identify this *black* butterfly by its narrow *red-brown border* and many *pale cream-white spots.* It has the typical *checkerspot* pattern below. You can find it in marshes, along streams, or on dry hillsides. It is found through much of the eastern U.S. and southern Canada. Adults visit flowers infrequently.

ANICIA CHECKERSPOT **$1\frac{1}{4}$ – $2\frac{1}{4}$ in.**

This butterfly is *black* above with pale *yellow spots*, and has the *red, black, and yellow checkerspot pattern* below. The butterflies in some western populations range from orange to yellow-orange. The butterfly is found in many habitats including oak woodland, desert slopes, and sagebrush-covered hills in the western mountains. Adults visit a wide variety of flowers including yellow composites.

QUESTION MARK **$2\frac{1}{4}$ - 3 in.**

This species belongs to a group of species called anglewings because of their *irregular wing outlines.* This species has a *silver "question mark"* in the center of its hindwing underside. The hindwing tails have a pale violet tip. You can find the Question Mark in woodlands throughout the eastern U.S. and southern Canada. There are 2 broods a year, a summer brood with black-hindwinged adults and an overwintering brood with orange-hindwinged adults. Adults usually feed on animal droppings and at sap flows.

SATYR ANGLEWING **2 – $2\frac{1}{2}$ in.**

This butterfly is golden brown above with a *dark spot* in the center of the hindwing. There is a *silver comma mark* in the center of the hindwing below. Look for the Satyr Anglewing in openings in dense woodlands, especially along streams, in the western U.S. and southern Canada. The adults favor sap flows and rotting fruit but may nectar on flowers.

BALTIMORE
ANICIA
CHECKERSPOT
male
QUESTION
MARK
SATYR
ANGLEWING

Tortoise Shells

Butterflies in this group, which includes the familiar Mourning Cloak, emerge from their chrysalids in late spring and overwinter, then mate and lay eggs the following spring.

COMPTON TORTOISE SHELL **2¾ – 3⅛ in.**

Identify this brown butterfly by its *irregular wing margins* and the single *white spots* on forewing and hindwing margins. Compton Tortoise Shell is found in woodland openings in the northeastern U.S. and southern and western Canada.

CALIFORNIA TORTOISE SHELL **2⅜ – 3⅛ in.**

This bright orange-brown butterfly has a *short tail* on the hindwing, irregular *black borders*, and a few *black marks* on the interior of the forewing. It is found in shrublands and meadows in the mountainous regions of the western U.S. and southwestern Canada. The California Tortoise Shell has huge population explosions and mass migrations, during which they travel as far as the Great Lakes and New England.

MOURNING CLOAK **3⅛ – 4 in.**

This familiar butterfly can be identified by its *purplish black* wings with their *broad yellow border* edged inwardly with tiny bright blue spots. The normal habitat of this butterfly is in woodland openings along streams, but they move around so much that they may be seen almost anywhere. In the fall, many Mourning Cloaks migrate south, but others overwinter in the north. Mourning Cloaks usually feed at sap flows, but occasionally visit flowers for nectar.

MILBERT'S TORTOISE SHELL **1⅞ – 2½ in.**

Identify this butterfly by the *black inner half* of the wings, the *orange outer half* and the trim *black borders*. It is usually found in open fields or meadows across the northern U.S. and southern Canada.

COMPTON
TORTOISE
SHELL
CALIFORNIA
TORTOISE
SHELL
MOURNING
CLOAK
MILBERT'S
TORTOISE
SHELL

RED ADMIRAL **2¼ – 3 in.**

This black butterfly can be identified by the *red-orange bar* across the forewing and the *red-orange border* on the hindwing. The Red Admiral is most often found in openings in river woods or wooded swamps, but the adults wander extensively. The butterflies are found throughout most of the U.S. and southern Canada. Red Admirals overwinter as adults and migrate to the southern U.S. Adults feed on animal droppings, sap flows, and flower nectar.

AMERICAN PAINTED LADY **2⅛ – 2⅝ in.**

This orange and black butterfly may be identified by the *2 large eyespots* on the underside of the hindwing. It is found in fields, roadsides, and a wide variety of open habitats. The American Painted Lady is found in most of the U.S. and southern Canada, but is common in the East and rare in most of the West. Adults visit a wide variety of flowers including milkweeds, dogbane, and yellow composites.

PAINTED LADY **2¼ – 2⅞ in.**

The orange-pink and black Painted Lady can be identified by the *4 small mainly black eyespots* on the margin of the hindwing. Look for Ladies in open deserts, fields, and roadsides. This butterfly is not a year-round resident north of Mexico, but during major migrations in spring and summer it colonizes much of the U.S. and southern Canada. It is most common in the southwestern U.S. Adults nectar at many flowers, especially yellow composites.

WEST COAST LADY **2 – 2¼ in.**

You can identify this orange and black butterfly by the row of *4 blue eyespots* on the hindwing. The West Coast Lady is found in suburban gardens, parks, and waste areas. It is most common in the Pacific Coast states, but is regular in the western U.S. and adjacent southwestern Canada. Adults nectar at flowers including red valerian, buckeye, and yellow composites.

RED
ADMIRAL
AMERICAN
PAINTED
LADY
PAINTED
LADY
WEST
COAST
LADY

BUCKEYE **1⅝ – 2¾ in.**

You can identify this *brown* butterfly by the *large eyespots* along the edges of the wings. There are 2 other related species in North America. Buckeyes are found along dry creek beds, open fields, dunes, and roadsides. They are resident across the southern U.S., where the adults overwinter, but they regularly move north and may reach southern Canada. Males perch and patrol dry streambeds or dirt roads in their search for suitable mates. Adults nectar at flowers such as tickseed and rabbitbrush.

VICEROY **2⅝ – 3¼ in.**

This mimic of the Monarch (see page 76) is orange, but has a *thin black stripe* across each wing and a *single row of small white dashes* in the black wing borders. Viceroys are found in open areas along streams or marshes. You can find them in much of the U.S. and southern Canada, except for the Pacific coast. Look for Viceroys from late spring to fall. Adults feed on animal droppings and sap flows but also visit flowers. The caterpillars feed on the leaves of willows and poplars.

RED-SPOTTED PURPLE and WHITE ADMIRAL **3 – 4 in.**

In the central and southern U.S., the Red-spotted Purple is black with *iridescent purplish blue* above and has a row of submarginal *red-orange spots* below. In the northeastern U.S., Canada, and Alaska, the White Admiral has white bands across the forewing and hindwing. There is a broad area across New England and the Great Lakes states where both varieties and their hybrids occur. The butterflies are found in sunny openings in a wide variety of woodlands. Adults feed on animal droppings and fermenting fruit and rarely visit flowers. The caterpillars feed on leaves of oaks, aspen, poplars, and wild cherry.

BUCKEYE
VICEROY
RED-SPOTTED
PURPLE
WHITE
ADMIRAL
RED-SPOTTED
PURPLE

LORQUIN'S ADMIRAL **2 – 2⅝ in.**

Identify this black butterfly by the *orange band* on the tip of the forewing and the *white band* across both wings. This butterfly is usually found in openings along streamsides. The Lorquin's Admiral is found in the western states and southwestern Canada. There are two flights in late spring and midsummer. Adults nectar at flowers such as buckeye and yerba santa but also feed on animal droppings. Caterpillars eat leaves of willows.

WEIDEMEYER'S ADMIRAL **2½ – 3¾ in.**

Also known as the Skunk, this black butterfly has a *white stripe* across each wing. Look for Weidemeyer's Admiral along streams in mountainous areas in the Rocky Mountains of the western U.S. and southern Canada. Adults visit flowers and feed on animal droppings. The caterpillars eat the leaves of willows, aspen, and cottonwood.

CALIFORNIA SISTER **2⅝ – 4 in.**

Identify this large black butterfly by the large, *black-edged orange patch* on the tip of the forewing and the narrow *white band* through the middle of each wing. The California Sister has a pronounced flap-and-glide flight. It is a butterfly of the Southwest, found near oak trees in oak woodland, pine-oak forest, or other forests with many oaks. You can find adults flying in late spring and again in late summer. Adults congregate at moist spots near streams and take nectar from flowers such as buckeye. Caterpillars eat leaves of oaks and tan oak.

LORQUIN'S
ADMIRAL
WEIDEMEYER'S
ADMIRAL
CALIFORNIA
SISTER

GOATWEED BUTTERFLY **2½ – 3¼ in.**

Identify this bright *orange-red* butterfly by its *sickle-shaped forewing tip* and the *pointed tail* on the trailing edge of the hindwing. This butterfly can be found in a wide range of habitats including river woods and scrubby woodland. It is resident in the Gulf states and regularly wanders inland in the mid-South and Southwest. Two broods emerge each year, one in midsummer and another in the fall that overwinters. Adults of the 2 flights have slighfly different markings and wing shapes. Goatweed Butterflies feed at sap flows and animal droppings. The caterpillars eat goatweed and other crotons.

HACKBERRY BUTTERFLY **1⅞ – 2½ in.**

The medium-sized Hackberry Butterfly can be identified by the *single eyespot* on the forewing and the series of small eyespots on the hindwing. It is found near hackberry trees in a wide variety of habitats including river woods, shelterbelts, parks, and desert canyons. It is found in most of the U.S. except for the northern Rocky Mountains and Pacific coast states, and it rarely reaches southern Canada. Adults visit sap flows and animal droppings. The caterpillars live and feed in groups on leaves of hackberry.

TAWNY EMPEROR **2 – 2¾ in.**

This variable butterfly is similar to the Hackberry Butterfly, but it has *2 dark bars* on the front edge of the forewing and *no forewing eyespots*. Look for it in woodland habitats, often near streams or rivers. It is resident in the Southeast and Southwest but regularly flies north to the northeastern U.S. and occasionally reaches southern Ontario. Adults feed at sap flows and animal droppings; they rarely visit flowers such as common milkweed. The caterpillars live in groups and feed on hackberry.

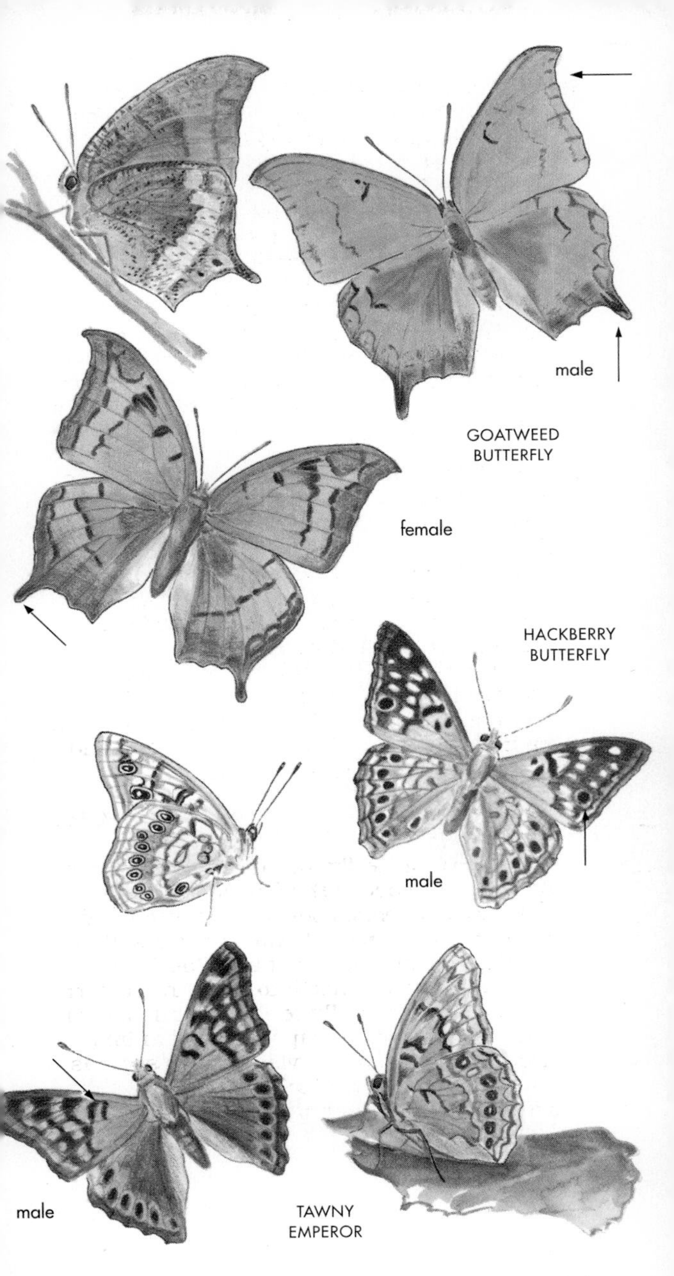
male
GOATWEED
BUTTERFLY
female
HACKBERRY
BUTTERFLY
male
male
TAWNY
EMPEROR

Satyrs

These members of the brushfoot family have swollen veins at the base of their wings. They are usually brown but may be orange or gray. Most species have eyespots. The caterpillars feed on grasses and related plants.

NORTHERN PEARLY EYE **2¼ – 2¾ in.**

This brown butterfly has a series of *large eyespots* along the edges of both wings and a *wavy hindwing margin.* You can find it in the eastern U.S. and southern Canada, in damp deciduous woods often near streams or marshes. Adults never visit flowers but feed at sap flows, rotting fruit, and animal droppings.

EYED BROWN **1¾ – 2½ in.**

Identify this soft brown butterfly by the series of *small round eyespots* near the wing margins and the *dark zigzag line* on the underside of each hindwing. The Eyed Brown inhabits open marshes and partially treed wetlands. It is found in the northern U.S. and southern Canada east of the Rocky Mountains. Adults feed at sap flows and bird droppings; they occasionally nectar at flowers.

MITCHELL'S SATYR **1⅜ – 1¾ in.**

This *endangered* butterfly can be identified by its small size and brown *translucent wings* and the series of *closely positioned round eyespots* on the undersides of the wings. Mitchell's Satyr is limited to a few wetlands in Michigan and North Carolina.

CAROLINA SATYR **1¼ – 1½ in.**

This small brown butterfly is common in much of the South. It has *small, well-spaced, yellow-rimmed marginal eyespots* on the undersides of both wings. Look for it in woods with grassy areas. The adults fly close to the forest floor and feed on bird droppings and other organic wastes. They overwinter in the Deep South and Texas.

NORTHERN
PEARLY EYE
EYED
BROWN
MITCHELL'S
SATYR
CAROLINA
SATYR

LITTLE WOOD SATYR **1⅝ – 1⅞ in.**

This common brown butterfly has *2 prominent eyespots* on each wing. It is found throughout the eastern half of the U.S. and southern Canada in woods and brushy areas. Adults feed on bird droppings or rotting fruit.

RINGLET **1¼ – 1½ in.**

The Ringlet usually has a *small, round, black eyespot* on the tip of the forewing below. The butterflies' color ranges from off-white to yellow to dark brown. Look for Ringlets on open grassy hillsides, swales, or moist meadows. It is found in the northern states, western mountains, and southern Canada. Adults nectar on low flowers.

RIDINGS' SATYR **1½ – 2 in.**

This gray butterfly has *2 black eyespots* on each forewing and a *series of cream or yellowish bars* on the middle part of both wings. There are no similar butterflies. You can find Ridings' Satyr on shortgrass prairies, or arid grasslands. As you walk through the grasslands you might mistake these butterflies for grasshoppers because of their sudden, low, jerky flight. The butterfly's range includes the western Great Plains and the intermountain western U.S.

COMMON WOOD NYMPH **1⅞ – 3 in.**

This medium to large brown butterfly is identified by the *2 large, yellow-rimmed eyespots* near the edge of each forewing. Common Wood Nymphs in the South have large yellow patches surrounding the eyespots. You can find this common butterfly in a wide variety of grassy areas, including abandoned fields, hillsides, and swales. The Common Wood Nymph is found through much of the U.S. and southern Canada but is rare or absent in the southwestern U.S. Adults occasionally nectar at flowers such as white sweet clover but more often feed on animal droppings or sap flows.

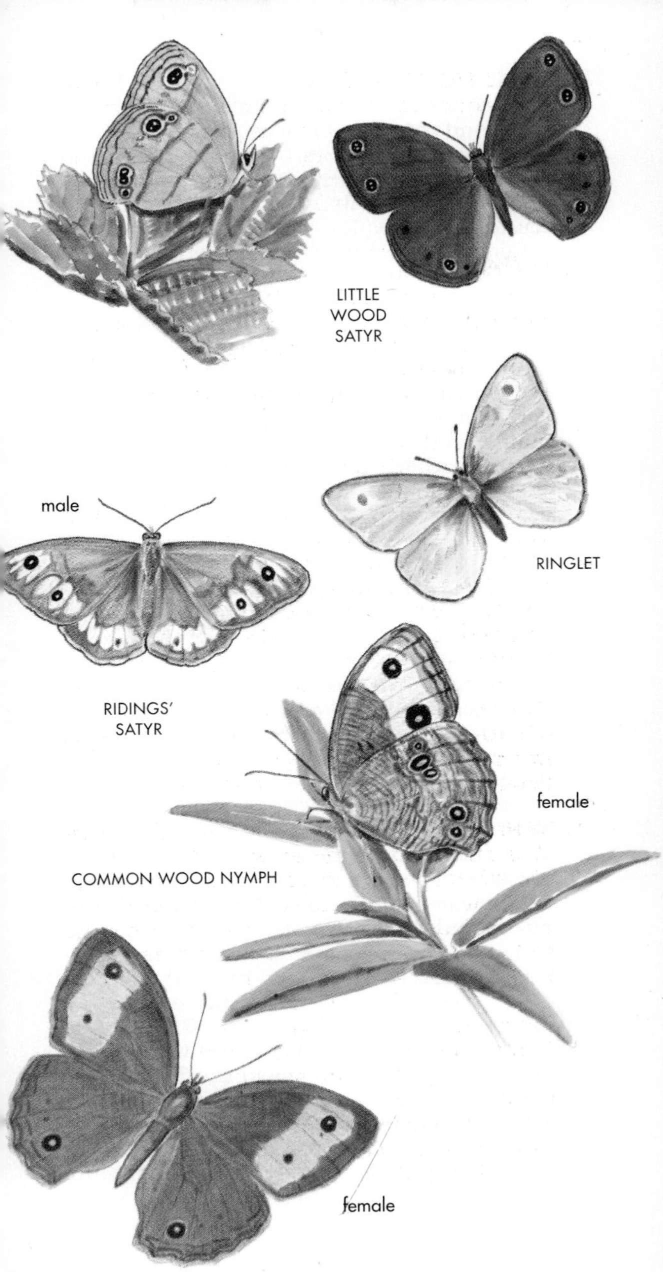
LITTLE
WOOD
SATYR
male
RINGLET
RIDINGS'
SATYR
female
COMMON WOOD NYMPH
female

COMMON ALPINE **1⅞ – 2 in.**

Identify this butterfly by its *black-brown* color and many small eyespots surrounded by *orange-red patches.* There are a number of other alpines in the Rocky Mountains, Canada, and Alaska. The Common Alpine is found in wet swales and meadows in mountains of the western U.S., western Canada, and Alaska. Adults feed on flower nectar.

CHRYXUS ARCTIC **1¾ – 2¼ in.**

Identify this orange butterfly by the *small marginal black eyespots* and the *gray mottled pattern* on the underside of the hindwings. It is found in high, rocky places, mainly in the western mountains but also in the northern Great Lakes and adjacent eastern Canada. This butterfly needs 2 years to develop from egg to adult.

Royalty

The big butterflies in this group of brushfoots all lay their eggs on milkweed plants.

MONARCH **3⅝ – 4⅞ in.**

Our best known butterfly is orange with *black veins* and a *black border with 2 rows of tiny white spots.* Males have a black scent patch on the hindwing. The Monarch is distasteful to birds, thanks to the toxins it acquires from the milkweeds it eats as a caterpillar. The Viceroy is an edible mimic of the Monarch. Monarchs can be found in a wide variety of open areas throughout the U.S. and southern Canada. In fall, Monarchs migrate south to overwinter in huge numbers at a few sites in coastal California and central Mexico.

QUEEN **3⅛ – 3⅞ in.**

The Queen looks like a *small, chocolate brown* Monarch. Viceroys in the South mimic Queens instead of Monarchs. Queens are found in open areas including desert scrub and grassy fields. The Queen is found in the southern U.S. and ranges south into the tropics. They occasionally wander north to the central U.S.

COMMON
ALPINE
CHRYXUS
ARCTIC
MONARCH
QUEEN

Skippers

Most skippers are small to medium orange or black butterflies. They have short, hooked, clubbed antennae, relatively stout bodies, and short wings, and they hold their wings open when at rest.

SILVER-SPOTTED SKIPPER **2 – 2⅝ in.**
This large dark brown skipper has a *metallic silver patch* on the underside of each hindwing and a *transparent gold patch* on each forewing. It is found in a variety of open habitats, such as brushy fields, in most of the U.S. and southern Canada. Adults are avid visitors to flowers such as milkweeds, thistles, and dogbane.

LONG-TAILED SKIPPER **1⅞ – 2¼ in.**
This butterfly can be identified by the *iridescent green* at the bases of its wings and the *long tail* on each hindwing. These butterflies can be found in open weedy fields and scrubby areas in the southern U.S. from Florida west to Arizona. Adults visit many flowers such as lantana and composites.

NORTHERN CLOUDY WING **1⅜ – 1¾ in.**
This dark brown butterfly has a few *triangular transparent spots* on the outer portion of the forewing. The underside of the hindwing is *mottled gray-brown*. Adults usually rest with their wings spread flat. Look for this butterfly in woodlands with small openings, in much of the U.S. and southern Canada except the Great Plains. Adults visit a variety of flowers including common milkweed, dogbane, self-heal, and red clover.

DREAMY DUSKY WING **1¼ – 1½ in.**
Dusky wings are among our most difficult butterflies to identify. This small black skipper has *long palps, lacks white spots*, and has *several gray bars* on the forewing. Look for it in openings or fields near moist forests in the northern U.S. and southern Canada. Adults visit flowers such as blueberry, wild strawberry, and purple vetch.

SILVER-SPOTTED
SKIPPER
LONG-TAILED
SKIPPER
NORTHERN
CLOUDY
WING
DREAMY
DUSKY WING

FUNEREAL DUSKY WING **1¼ – 1¾ in.**
This brown-black skipper has long forewings, a small *red-brown patch* on the forewing, and *white hindwing fringes*. Several other western dusky wings also have white hindwing fringes. You can find the Funereal Dusky Wing in arid canyons, desert scrub, and weedy fields. Its range includes most of the Southwest and extends to the Gulf Coast. Adults are avid flower visitors, nectaring on a wide variety of flowers.

CHECKERED SKIPPER **1¼ – 1½ in.**
This is a small, black and white checkered butterfly that rests near the ground with wings spread open. The Checkered Skipper can be found in a wide variety of open habitats, including weedy fields, lawns, and desert washes. You can find it in most of the U.S. and southern Canada. Adults take nectar from many flowers including clovers, asters, and knapweed.

COMMON SOOTY WING **1 – 1¼ in.**
This is a small, glossy black skipper with small white spots on the forewing. You can find this common butterfly in a wide variety of open, sunny habitats including weedy fields, road edges, and vacant lots. The species is found in most of the U.S. and occasionally in southern Canada. Adults fly very close to the ground and take nectar from a variety of low flowers including white clover, dogbane, and marjoram.

LEAST SKIPPER **⅞ – 1⅛ in.**
You can identify this small, weak-flying skipper by its *black forewing* and the *black marginal band* on its orange hindwing. Look for the Least Skipper in wet, grassy areas and marshes. The butterfly is found in the eastern half of the U.S. and southern Canada. The adults visit low flowers such as mist flower, pickerelweed, and buttonbush.

FUNEREAL
DUSKY
WING
CHECKERED
SKIPPER
COMMON
SOOTY
WING
LEAST SKIPPER

FIERY SKIPPER **1¼ – 1½ in.**

Identify this skipper by the *small black dots* on the underside of the hindwing. Above, the male is mostly bright yellow-orange with a black slash on the front wing and a jagged black border on the hindwing. The female is mainly brown above. Look for these butterflies in yards, parks, or gardens. This skipper is found across the southern U.S. and travels north in summer or fall. The adults visit flowers including lantana, marigold, verbena, and vinca.

COMMON BRANDED SKIPPER **1⅛ – 1½ in.**

This butterfly is orange with *white or silvery spots* on the underside of the hindwing in most areas. You can find it in mostly undisturbed habitats including brushy foothills with grassy openings, oak woodlands, and sagebrush flats. The skipper ranges from southern Canada west to the Pacific Coast, south in the western mountains, and north to Alaska. Adults visit flowers including aster, thistles, and white sweet clover.

PECK'S SKIPPER **1 – 1¼ in.**

This skipper is easily identified by the central *patch of yellow spots* on the underside of the hindwing. It is found in grassy meadows, roadsides, and suburban parks and lawns across the northern and central states and southern Canada. The adults take nectar from a variety of flowers including marigolds and self-heal.

HOBOMOK SKIPPER **1½ – 1¾ in.**

The male is yellow-orange with irregular black borders and *lacks a black stigma.* The female has 2 forms, a yellow-orange form similar to the male but duller, and a dark form that is purplish black. The Hobomok Skipper is found in openings in deciduous woods or near streams or rivers, in the northeastern U.S. and adjacent southern Canada and in a few spots in the southern Rockies. Adults nectar at several flowers including dame's rocket and small mints.

male
FIERY
SKIPPER
male
male
COMMON BRANDED SKIPPER
female
PECK'S
SKIPPER
dark
female
male
HOBOMOK
SKIPPER

DION SKIPPER **1½ – 1¾ in.**

This dark skipper can be identified by the 2 *yellow rays* that cross the underside of the orange-brown hindwing. This butterfly is found in marshes or openings in wooded swamps in the eastern U.S. and adjacent southern Canada. Adults visit flowers such as buttonbush or pickerelweed.

SACHEM **1⅜ – 1⅝ in.**

The orangish male can be identified by the *4-sided black marking* on the upperside of the forewing, while the large, more brownish female can be identified by the *transparent forewing patch.* The Sachem is found in a wide variety of weedy or disturbed habitats. It is found over the southern and central U.S. and occasionally wanders north to Canada. The adults can be seen nectaring at many flowers including alfalfa, marigolds, verbena, and chrysanthemums.

BRAZILIAN SKIPPER **2 – 2⅜ in.**

This large, dark, tropical skipper has *large translucent spots* on the pointed forewing and *cream spots* on the underside of the red-brown hindwing. Look for the butterfly in gardens or in wet tropical woods. The Brazilian Skipper is resident in south Florida and south Texas but may range north to the central U.S. on rare occasions. It is found year-round in subtropical areas that never freeze.

YUCCA SKIPPER **1⅞ – 3⅛ in.**

On the upperside, this very large, robust skipper has a *yellow band* on the outer part of the forewing and a *yellow marginal band* on the hindwing. The hindwing is *gray* below. The Yucca Skipper is always found in habitats with yuccas; these range from openings in pine woods to desert canyons and arid plains. The Yucca Skipper is found across the southern U.S. Adults do not visit flowers but may be seen imbibing moisture at wet spots near streams or gullies.

DION
SKIPPER
male
male
female
SACHEM
BRAZILIAN
SKIPPER
YUCCA
SKIPPER

Moths

There are about 15 times more kinds of moths than butterflies. Most species are dull-colored and fly at night, but many are brightly colored, and many fly during the day.

Micro Moths

These are the most primitive moth species. Although most species are small or even tiny, some are very large.

SILVER-SPOTTED GHOST MOTH **2½ – 4 in.**

Ghost moths fly at dusk and are rarely attracted to lights. This large moth has a slightly hooked, gray to tan forewing crossed by irregular dark bands. Look for it at dusk along streamsides lined with alders. The moth is found in the Northeast and southern Canada, west to North Dakota.

YUCCA MOTH **½ – 1¼ in.**

This small *white* moth with a *gray, white-fringed* hindwing is completely dependent on the yucca for food, and the yucca is completely dependent on the moth for pollination. The female moth lays her eggs inside the yucca flower, then gathers a ball of yucca pollen and places it on the stigma of a yucca flower, pollinating it. When the larvae hatch, they eat the seeds in the yucca pod, but leave enough seeds to ensure the next generation of yucca plants. The adults' emergence is exactly timed to the local blooming schedule of the yuccas.

THREE-BANDED FAIRY MOTH **⅜ – ⅝ in.**

This common day-flying moth is found primarily in California. It is mainly black with *long white antennae,* 3 times as long as the forewing. Males have 3 white bands across the forewing, and females have yellow bands and orange scales on the head. The moths hover with slowly whirling antennae or rest on small yellow flowers on grassy hillsides in California's oak-covered foothills.

SILVER-SPOTTED
GHOST MOTH
YUCCA
MOTH
THREE-BANDED
FAIRY MOTH

EVERGREEN BAGWORM MOTH **¾ – 1½ in.**

The male moth has brownish, *transparent wings*. The caterpillars live in silk bags shingled with small twigs on their host plants, especially eastern redcedar. The wingless female never leaves her bag. The bags are found in open woodlands from the eastern U.S. west to the Great Plains.

GOLDENROD GALL MOTH **⅞ – 1 in.**

This gray moth belongs to the gelechioid superfamily, the second largest group of moths. Most are small and brown or gray. The forewing of the Goldenrod Gall Moth is gray, gray-brown, and white with a *curved black patch* that is edged in white along its bottom. The species is found in open fields, roadsides, and along railroad tracks. It is found mainly in eastern North America. The adults fly in late summer or fall. The larvae cause spherical galls on the stems of goldenrods.

MANY-PLUME MOTH **½ – ⅝ in.**

Each wing of this tiny moth is divided into *6 fingerlike plumes* almost to the base. The moth is found in a wide variety of natural and disturbed habitats, mainly in the northern U.S. and southern Canada. It flies in the spring and early summer.

AILANTHUS WEBWORM MOTH **¾ – 1¼ in.**

The Ailanthus Webworm Moth is a member of the Ermine Moth family. The forewings are orange with *4 rows of small, black-outlined yellow spots*. This moth is usually found in suburban habitats but is also found in mesquite scrub and deserts. It is very common in the eastern U.S. but ranges across the southern states. You can find the moths from spring to midsummer. They are active during the day but also are attracted to lights at night. The larvae form large communal webs at the ends of branches on ailanthus, paradise tree, and related plants.

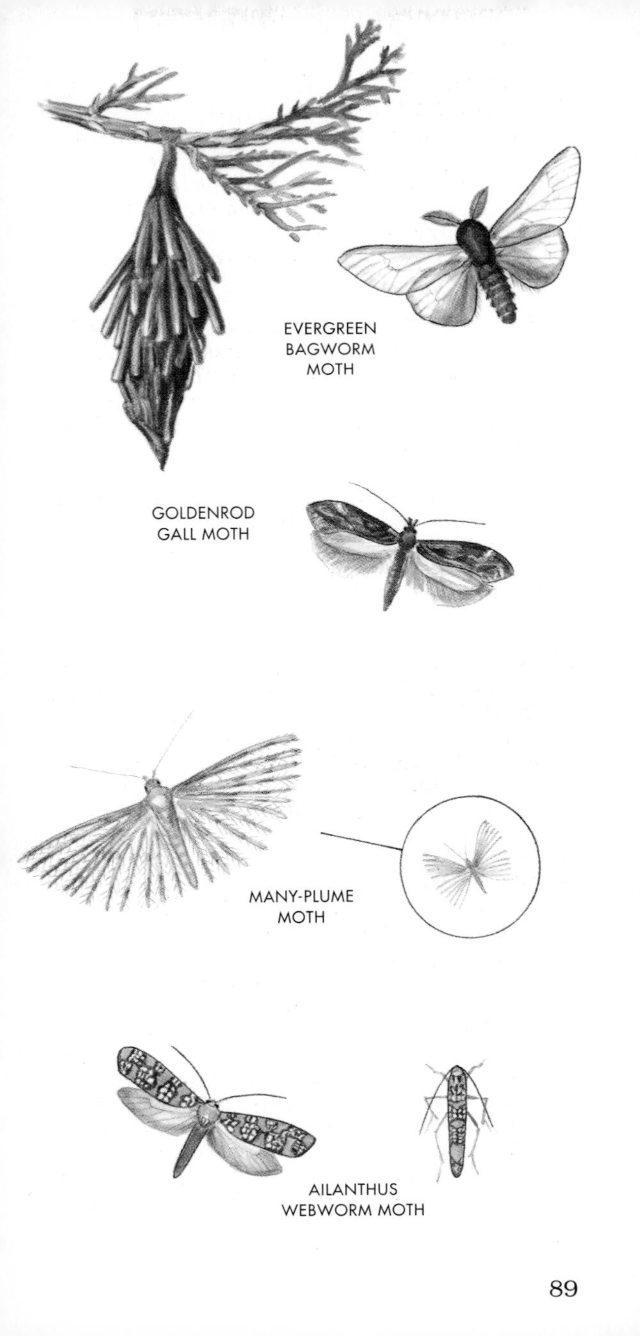
EVERGREEN
BAGWORM
MOTH
GOLDENROD
GALL MOTH
MANY-PLUME
MOTH
AILANTHUS
WEBWORM MOTH

HORNET CLEARWING **1¼ – 1¾**

This is one of many species in the clear-winged moth family that looks and flies very much like a large yellow and black hornet. It is black with yellow markings. The abdomen is *yellow wlth a black basal area crossed by yellow.* It is found in or near deciduous forests. The adults fly in late spring.

SQUASH VINE BORER MOTH **1 – 1¼ in.**

This common garden pest is identified by its *dark green forewings* and *bright orange, black-spotted abdomen.* It is found in suburban areas, especially near gardens. The moth is most common in the eastern U.S. and southern Canada. The adults may be found from spring to fall flying during the day and nectaring at plants such as dogbane and milkweeds. The caterpillars cause considerable damage to squash, gourds, and pumpkins.

CODLING MOTH **⅝ – ⅞ in.**

This common pest of apples is identified by its *striated gray forewing* with an oval, *shiny brown patch* on the outer third. The moths are found in orchards and suburban areas throughout most of the U.S. and southern Canada. The adults are active at night. The larvae bore into and feed on the fruits of apples, pears, walnuts, and other trees.

CARPENTERWORM MOTH **1¾ – 3⅜ in.**

This is a large, robust moth with thin scales. The males have a gray forewing and a *black-bordered orange hindwing.* The female's forewing is translucent *gray with black mottling.* You can find Carpenterworm Moths near wooded areas in a wide variety of habitats throughout most of North America. The adults fly primarily in midsummer. They are attracted to light and do not visit flowers.

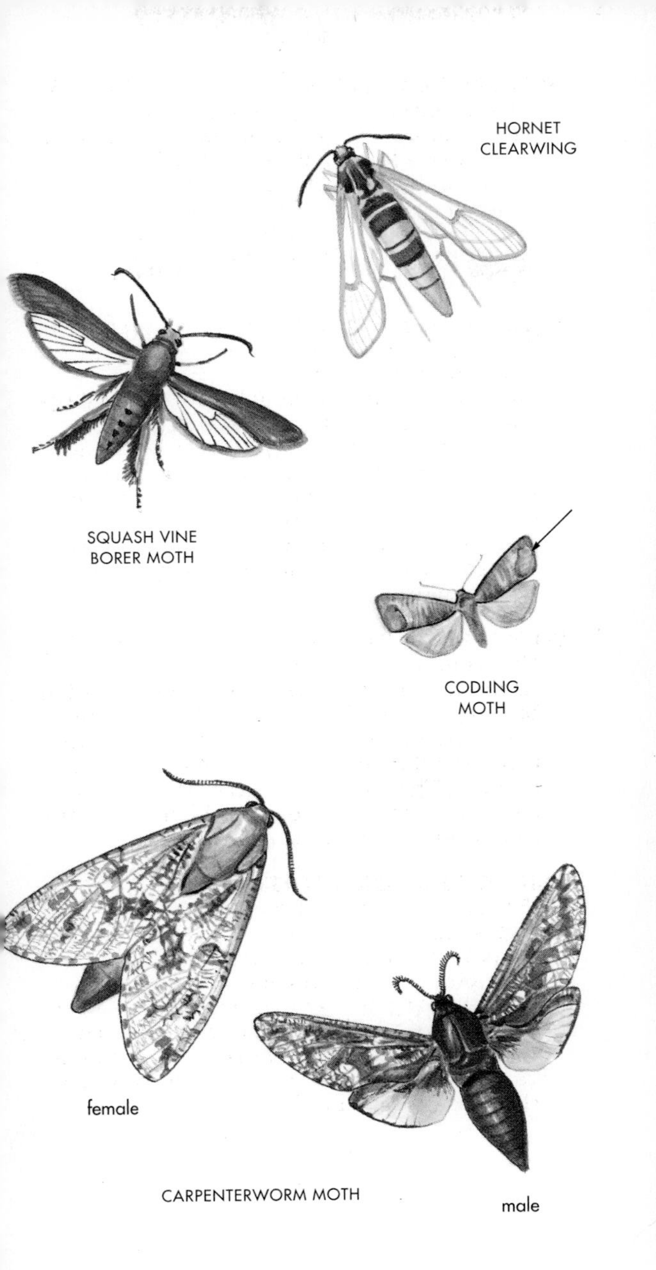
HORNET
CLEARWING
SQUASH VINE
BORER MOTH
CODLING
MOTH
female
CARPENTERWORM MOTH
male

WESTERN SPRUCE BUDWORM MOTH — **⅞ – 1¼ in.**

The forewing of the Western Spruce Budworm Moth is *mottled orange, gray, or brown,* and the hindwing is gray. It is found in conifer forests in the western U.S. and adjacent parts of southern Canada. The adults fly in midsummer. The larvae feed on the needles of conifers such as Douglas-fir, firs, and spruce. When they occur in huge numbers, the larvae can strip all the conifers in a large area.

SMALLER PARASA — **¾ – 1⅛ in.**

Identify this moth by its *green thorax* and the brown forewing with a *green patch* that has a nearly straight outer edge. Look for the Smaller Parasa in or near deciduous woodlands or scrubby fields in the eastern U.S. The larvae, called Saddleback Caterpillars, have stinging hairs. They feed on the leaves of woody plants such as dogwoods, elms, apple, and oaks.

GRAPE LEAFFOLDER MOTH — **¾ – 1⅛ in.**

This small, black moth has pointed forewings with *2 white spots* and a larger white spot on each hindwing. The Grape Leaffolder is found in a variety of open, brushy habitats. It is found in the eastern U.S., adjacent southern Canada, and the southwestern U.S. The caterpillars make shelters out of a folded leaf, and they eat the leaves of both wild and domestic grapevines.

PLUME MOTH — **¾ – 1⅛ in.**

There are dozens of plume moth species in North America. Most have each hindwing divided into *3 plumelike parts.* They are mainly found in suburban areas, meadows, and fields.

WESTERN SPRUCE
BUDWORM MOTH

orange form

brown form

SMALLER
PARASA

GRAPE
LEAFFOLDER
MOTH

PLUME
MOTH

Macro Moths

Macro moths, or "Macrolepidoptera," include the advanced groups of moths. Most species are medium to large in size. A few have caterpillars that bore into plants to feed.

LETTERED HABROSYNE **1⅓ – 1½ in.**

This moth has gray-brown wings. The forewings have several *white lines or bars accented with pink.* Look for Lettered Habrosynes in open habitats, including suburban gardens, over most of the U.S. and southern Canada.

ARCHED HOOKTIP **1 – 1½ in.**

Identify this medium-sized moth by the forewing with the *arched tip.* The wings are pale yellow-white to orange-yellow with *fine dark lines.* The moths are found in forested areas in the eastern U.S. and adjacent portions of southern Canada.

Inchworm or Geometer Moths

Geometer means "measure the earth." Geometers are named for the way the caterpillars move, moving forward with a loop in the middle. They do this because they have no legs on their middle segments. The adults of most species rest with their wings flat. Some species have wingless female adults.

FALL CANKERWORM MOTH **1 – 1¼ in.**

The males of this medium-sized moth have *translucent, gray, mottled wings.* The females are *wingless.* Fall Cankerworm Moths are found in suburban and forested habitats throughout most of the U.S. and southern Canada. The adults fly in fall and winter and are attracted to lights.

TULIP-TREE BEAUTY **1¾ – 2¼ in.**

This large geometer is mottled gray with *scalloped hindwing edges.* There are usually *black zigzag lines* across the wings. When the moth is at rest on a tree trunk, the wings blend perfectly against the bark. Look for Tulip-tree Beauties in moist deciduous forests in the eastern U.S.

LETTERED
HABROSYNE

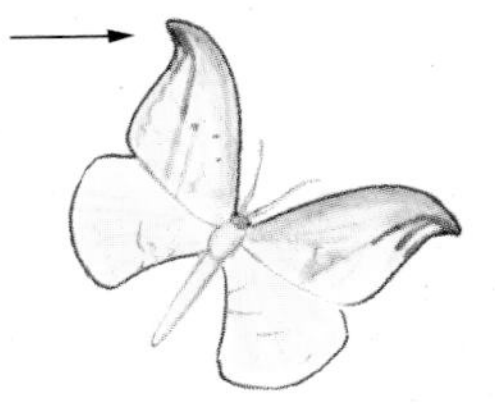

ARCHED
HOOKTIP

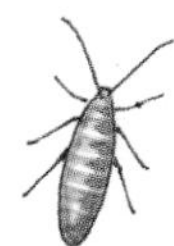

male

female

FALL
CANKERWORM
MOTH

TULIP-TREE
BEAUTY

PEPPER-AND-SALT GEOMETER **1½ – 1¾ in.**

This stout-bodied moth usually has gray wings marked with *wavy black lines.* A form with *black wings* found in industrial regions is protected from birds when it rests on soot-covered tree trunks. Look for this moth in forested areas in most of the northern U.S. and southern Canada.

INDIAN BLANKET MOTH **1⅛ – 1⅝ in.**

This medium-sized moth has *red-orange forewings* with *scattered white bars and dashes.* It is found in conifer forests of western foothills. The caterpillars eat the needles of several conifers.

ROSE-TOUCHED GREEN **1⅛ – 1½ in.**

This moth has a *narrow red border* on the inner edge of the hindwing. Look for it in pinyon forest or pine-oak canyons in the Southwest.

LAPPET MOTH **1¼ – 1⅞ in.**

The Lappet Moth holds its wings folded over its back like a tent when at rest. The forewings are usually *red-brown* with some black marks or smudges. The hindwings are blackish. The outer edges of both wings are *slightly scalloped.* You can find this species over most of the U.S. and southern Canada.

EASTERN TENT CATERPILLAR MOTH **⅞ – 1¾ in.**

The brown wings with *2 parallel white lines* across the forewing help identify this moth. Sometimes the area between the lines is filled with white. You can find the moths in suburban areas, brushy fields, and forest edges in the eastern half of the U.S. and adjacent portions of southern Canada. The caterpillars live in masses in white silken tents, but they leave the tents to feed. They eat many broad-leafed trees and shrubs, but apple and cherry are the most frequent food plants.

black form
PEPPER-AND-SALT
GEOMETER
INDIAN
BLANKET MOTH
ROSE-TOUCHED
GREEN
LAPPET MOTH
EASTERN TENT
CATERPILLAR MOTH

Giant Silkworm Moths

These large moths are among the most familiar moth species. Most are colorful. Like many female moths, most giant silkworm moths use chemical attractants ("pheromones") to advertise for mates, and the males home in using their feathery antennae as sensors. The adults do not feed and are short-lived. The caterpillars have bunches of bristly hairs; the hairs of some species can sting if touched. The cocoons are large and papery, and have been experimented with unsuccessfully in the past as a possible commercial source of silk. The Asian Silkworm Moth, which is raised for its silk, is in a different family that is not native to North America. These beautiful, large moths have declined or disappeared in some areas of eastern North America.

IMPERIAL MOTH **3¼–7 in.**

This magnificent moth is *yellow with pink, orange, or purplish brown flecks, spots, and patches.* The moth is a denizen of rich deciduous forests in the eastern U.S. and extreme southern Canada. The caterpillars eat the leaves of a variety of forest trees.

REGAL MOTH **3¾–6 in.**

The forewing of this spectacular moth is *gray with red-orange veins and yellow spots between the veins.* Regal Moths are found in suburban areas and in or near forests in the eastern U.S. The adults have a single midsummer flight and are attracted to lights. The caterpillar, known as the Hickory Horned Devil, eats the leaves of hickories and on occasion those of other broad-leafed plants.

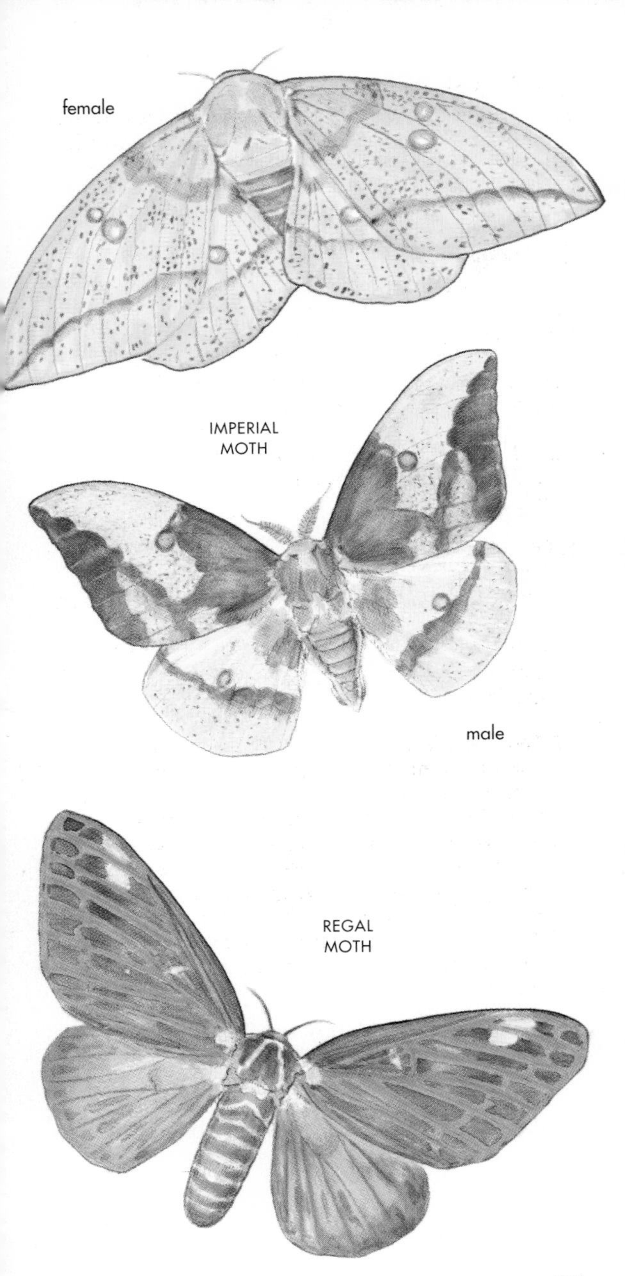
female
IMPERIAL
MOTH
male
REGAL
MOTH

ROSY MAPLE MOTH **1¼ – 2 in.**

You can easily identify this moth by its *rose and cream banded wings.* An all-white form is found on the eastern Great Plains. Look for the moth at lights in or near forests and in suburbs. It is found in the eastern U.S. and adjacent areas of Canada.

NEVADA BUCK MOTH **2 – 3 in.**

This moth can be identified by its wings' *broad black borders* and white central areas, each with a black spot. The abdomen is *black with a red-orange tip.* The Nevada Buck Moth is found near willows in arid regions of the western U.S. The moths fly near midday in the fall. The caterpillars have stinging spines and feed on willow leaves.

IO MOTH **2 – 3¼ in.**

The Io Moth has yellow hindwings, each with a *large, blue-black, white-centered eyespot.* When the moth is at rest, the hindwing is normally hidden, but when disturbed the moth flashes its bright hindwing and eyespot — a sight that might frighten and discourage a would-be predator. The Io Moth is found in a variety of habitats including suburban gardens, deciduous forests, and mesquite scrub. You can find Io Moths over the eastern U.S. west to the Rocky Mountains and in parts of southeastern Canada. The caterpillars have stinging spines.

COMMON SHEEP MOTH **2½ – 3¼ in.**

The Common Sheep Moth has *pink forewings* and *yellow-orange hindwings* that look like they were written on with a black crayon. Some forms in northern California are almost completely black. The Sheep Moth is found in brushy habitats near streams in much of the western U.S. The caterpillars have stinging hairs and eat leaves of a wide variety of shrubs including wild rose and wild lilacs.

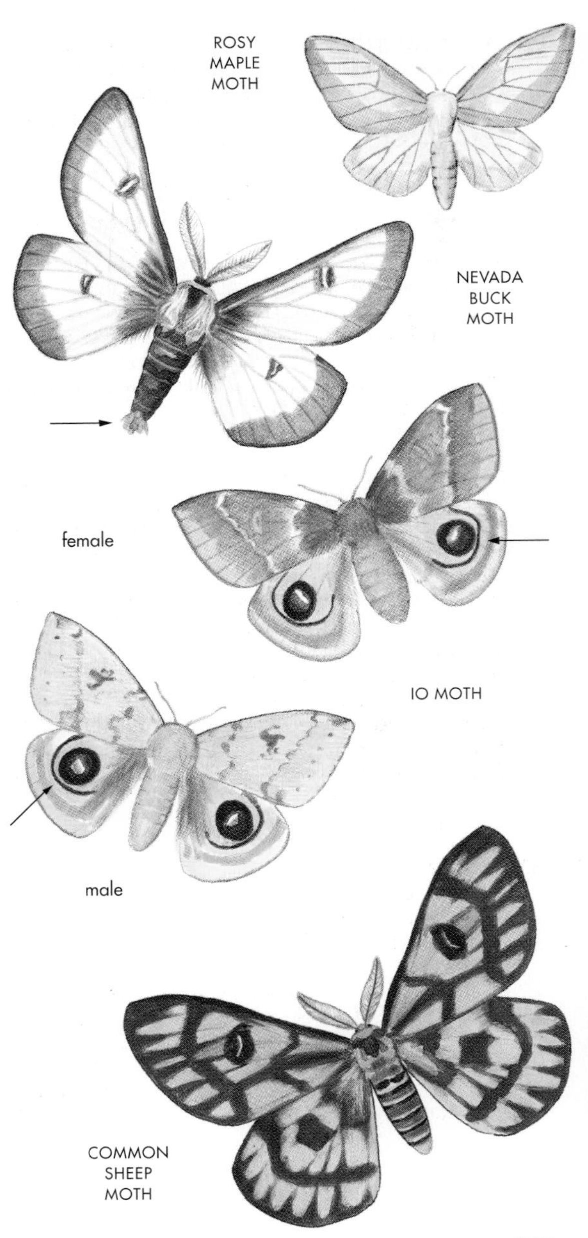
ROSY
MAPLE
MOTH
NEVADA
BUCK
MOTH
female
IO MOTH
male
COMMON
SHEEP
MOTH

POLYPHEMUS MOTH **4 – 6 in.**

This common moth has sandy tan to orange-tan wings and feathery antennae. Each forewing has a *small transparent eyespot,* and each hindwing has a *large transparent eyespot* connected to a *large blue-black patch.* These eyespots inspired the Polyphemus's name; it is named for a one-eyed giant of Greek mythology. You can find these moths in a wide variety of habitats ranging from suburban yards to desert canyons and deciduous forests. The range of the Polyphemus Moth includes most of the U.S. and southern Canada. The caterpillars have been found to eat the leaves of more than 50 kinds of broad-leafed trees and shrubs.

LUNA MOTH **3 – 4⅛ in.**

The Luna is probably our most familiar and most spectacular moth. It has *pale green* wings and a *long, curved tail* on each hindwing. There is also a small eyespot on each wing. Look for the Luna Moth in rich deciduous forests in the eastern U.S. and southern Canada. Polyphemus Moths are readily attracted to lights. The caterpillars eat the leaves of many different broad-leafed trees. In Canada, the caterpillars feed mainly on white birch, but farther south they feed most often on hickories.

POLYPHEMUS
MOTH
LUNA MOTH

CECROPIA MOTH **4¼ – 6 in.**

You can identify the Cecropia, also called the Robin Moth, by its dark gray wings with *teardrop-shaped, red-orange and white marks* on the middle of each wing and the *red-orange and white bands* across each wing. There are several similar relatives in different parts of the U.S. and Canada. Look for the Cecropia Moth in forests and suburban habitats. It ranges throughout the U.S. and Canada east of the Rockies. The moths are attracted to lights. The caterpillars feed on the leaves of many broad-leafed trees and shrubs.

PROMETHEA MOTH **3 – 3¾ in.**

The sexes of this moth are marked and colored quite differently. Above, the male is dark purplish brown with a *tan border* and a *faint white line* through each wing. The female is reddish orange to brown with a *white spot, white line, and narrow tan border* on each wing. Look for the moths in deciduous forests. They are found throughout the eastern U.S. and adjacent portions of southern Canada. You can find the males flying in late afternoon and the females at night. Mating takes place at dusk. The caterplllars feed on a wide variety of trees, but spicebush, sassafras, yellow poplar, and wild cherry are their preferred food plants.

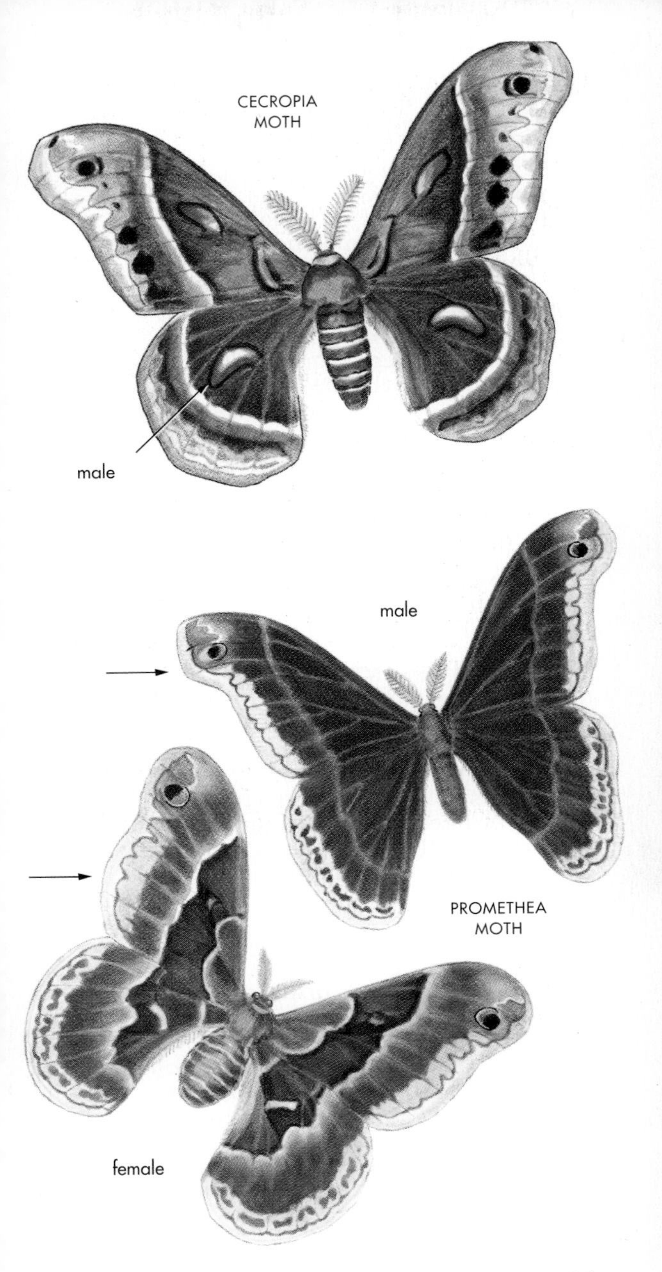
CECROPIA
MOTH
male
male
PROMETHEA
MOTH
female

Sphinx or Hawk Moths

These are robust, swift-flying moths that often hover in front of flowers, from which they suck nectar with their long, coiled probosces, which they extend while hovering. Most species fly at night and are attracted to flowers such as petunias and nicotiana and to lights. A few species fly only in the day.

CAROLINA SPHINX **4¼ – 5 in.**

This large gray moth with white and black mottling has *5 prominent yellow-orange spots* along each side of the abdomen. The moths are found in open habitats including farmland, suburbs, and scrubby areas. The Carolina Sphinx resides across the southern U.S., and it invades and colonizes more northern states in the summer and fall. The adults fly all year in Florida. The caterpillar, known as the Tobacco Hornworm, feeds on tobacco, tomato, and potato plants, as does the Tomato Hornworm, caterpillar of the similar Five-spotted Hawk Moth.

ONE-EYED SPHINX **2½ – 3⅜ in.**

This common sphinx has a scalloped tan or dark gray forewing. The hindwing is *pink* with a *black and blue eyespot.* Look for the One-eyed Sphinx in a variety of habitats such as suburbs, along streams, and in nearby forests, from the northeastern U.S. across southern Canada and throughout the western U.S. mountains and lowlands.

BIG POPLAR SHINX **4 – 4¾ in.**

Identify this moth by the green-brown or gray-brown forewing with a scalloped outer edge. The *outer ⅔ is distinctly darker.* The hindwing is red and gray with a *black triangular patch* at the corner. Look for the moth near cottonwoods in moist river woods or mountain streams. The moth ranges from the eastern U.S. and southern Canada across the continent and south in the western mountains. It is absent or very rare in the Southwest, where the similar but paler Western Poplar Sphinx occurs.

CAROLINA
SPHINX
ONE-EYED
SPHINX
BIG POPLAR SPHINX

HUMMINGBIRD CLEARWING **1¾–2¾ in.**

You may see this moth hovering in front of flowers, sucking nectar like a hummingbird. It has *transparent wings* bordered with dark brown. Look for this moth during the daytime in fields, meadows, and other open areas. The moth is found in the eastern U.S., Canada, and west to the eastern Great Plains; it is also found in Oregon and north to Alaska. The caterpillars eat the leaves of viburnum, cherries, plum, honeysuckle, and snowberry.

NESSUS SPHINX **1½–2¼ in.**

The moths can be identified by their *reddish brown wings* and the *yellow-banded abdomen.* The Nessus Sphinx is found in suburbs and woodlands, usually near streams, from the eastern U.S. and adjacent southern Canada west to the base of the Rocky Mountains in Colorado. The adults fly in late afternoon or at dusk and feed at flowers such as lilacs and milkweeds.

WHITE-LINED SPHINX **2½–3⅝ in.**

This is our most widespread, abundant sphinx moth. Identify it by its brown forewing with diagonal yellow-tan bar and *white-lined veins,* together with the *red-pink band* across the hindwing. The abdomen has a series of *alternating black and white spots* along each side. You can find the White-lined Sphinx in almost any open habitat, including gardens, deserts, roadsides, and fields. The moth is resident in the South and invades and colonizes all of the U.S. and most of southern Canada every summer. The adults fly in the afternoon and at night and visit many kinds of flowers for nectar. You can find the caterpillars on a wide variety of plants.

HUMMINGBIRD
CLEARWING
NESSUS
SPHINX
WHITE-LINED
SPHINX

WILLOW TENTMAKER **1⅛ – 1½ in.**

This moth has gray wings with reddish shading and a *thin diagonal white line.* The adults rest with their wings in a tentlike position. The moth is found throughout the western U.S. The adults are attracted to lights. The caterpillars live in nests on willows and cottonwoods.

YELLOW-NECKED CATERPILLAR MOTH **1⅜ – 2⅛ in.**

The forewings are tan to orangish brown with *parallel thin dark lines,* and the top of the thorax is *dark red-brown.* The moth is found in forested habitats throughout the eastern U.S. and parts of southern Canada. When disturbed, the caterpillars arch their front and back ends up into a C shape.

Tiger Moths

Most tiger moths are furry and brilliantly colored with red, yellow, white, and black. The bright colors advertise their distastefulness to would-be predators such as birds. The banded Woolly Bear caterpillar is the larva of the Isabella Tiger Moth (not shown).

BLACK-AND-YELLOW LICHEN MOTH **1 – 1¼ in.**

This day-flying moth can be identified by its black wings with *yellow-orange wing bases.* The moths are found in a variety of woodland and open habitats, often near streams. This species is found in much of the eastern U.S. and adjacent southern Canada west to the Rocky Mountains. It flies during the day in summer and fall and can be found at flowers such as goldenrods, rabbitbrush, and dogbane. The caterpillars eat lichens.

BELLA MOTH **1 – 1¼ in.**

Identify this beauty by the pink and yellow forewing with *rows of white-edged black dots.* The hindwing is red-pink with an irregular black border. The moths are found during the day in open fields and road edges. You can find it in south Florida and south Texas.

WILLOW TENTMAKER

YELLOW-NECKED CATERPILLAR MOTH

BLACK-AND-YELLOW LICHEN MOTH

BELLA MOTH

SALT MARSH MOTH **1¾ – 2¾ in.**

Identify this common moth by the *black-spotted white wings* and the *yellow-orange, black-marked abdomen.* The hindwing of the male is orange. When threatened, the moth curls up and lies still, displaying its bright abdomen. Look for the Salt Marsh Moth in croplands, suburban gardens, marshes, open fields, roadsides, and foothlll canyons throughout the U.S. and southern Canada.

PAINTED TIGER MOTH **⅞ – 1½ in.**

This lovely moth has gray forewings with *pale wavy lines.* The hindwing and abdomen are *pink with gray patches.* Look for this species in a variety of habitats in the southwestern U.S., ranging from foothill canyons to brushy flats along streams.

VIRGIN TIGER MOTH **1¾ – 2¾ in.**

The black forewings of this common moth are *crisscrossed by cream lines,* and the hindwings are *red-pink* with *irregular black patches.* There are many more or less similar moths in North America. You can find these common moths in a variety of open habitats through much of the eastern U.S. and southern Canada.

SPOTTED TUSSOCK MOTH **1¼ – 1¾ in.**

The slightly pointed forewing is *yellow* and is crossed by *irregular brown bands.* The Spotted Tussock Moth is found in suburbs and other open habitats across the northern U.S. and southern Canada. It is found farther south in the western mountains.

SALT
MARSH
MOTH
female
male
PAINTED
TIGER
MOTH
VIRGIN
TIGER
MOTH
SPOTTED
TUSSOCK
MOTH

VIRGINIA CTENUCHA **1¾ – 2 in.**

This moth's head and "collar" are *orange*, while the abdomen is *metallic blue*. The forewing is gray brown, and the hindwings are black with *metallic blue at the base*. You can usually find this day-flying, wasplike moth in open fields or marshes. The moth ranges through the northeastern U.S. and adjacent southern Canada west to the eastern part of the Great Plains. The caterpillars feed on grasses, irises, and sedges.

DOUGLAS-FIR TUSSOCK MOTH **1 – 1¼ in.**

The males have rounded dark gray forewings, red-brown hindwings and feathery antennae, while the females are wingless. This species is found in conifer forests in the mountains of the western U.S. The caterpillars can be serious forest pests, defoliating firs and Douglas-firs.

GYPSY MOTH **1¼ – 2¾ in.**

The sexes of the Gypsy Moth are quite different in size, color, and markings. The male is much smaller and darker than the female and has feathery antennae. He is brown or tan with wavy black lines and a black spot on the forewing. The female is much larger and lighter, with filamentlike antennae and black-marked white wings. The female cannot fly. She lays huge masses of eggs on tree trunks and other objects. Around 1868, the Gypsy Moth was accidentally introduced into New England and has since spread over large areas of the eastern U.S. The caterpillars defoliate many kinds of trees, especially apples, cherries, oaks, and willows. Large areas of forest may be stripped, and eventually the composition of the forest changes. The effects of Gypsy Moth feeding, combined with pesticides intended for Gypsy Moths, may have seriously reduced the populations of other eastern moths.

VIRGINIA
CTENUCHA
female
male
DOUGLAS-FIR
TUSSOCK MOTH
male
GYPSY
MOTH
female
egg mass

Owlet Moths

These moths, also known as noctuids and millers (because they look as if they have been dusted with flour), are the largest North American moth group. The adults are small to large. Most species are gray or brown and fly at night, but there are some brightly colored species and some that are strictly day-fliers. The caterpillars of some species, known as cutworms or armyworms, can damage crops and grazing lands.

BLACK WITCH **4¼ – 6 in.**

This is a *huge* brown-black moth with an eyespot on each forewing. There is an *oval patch with 2 spots* on the edge of each hindwing. The usual habitats of the Black Witch are tropical woods and suburbs in southern Florida, south Texas, and southern California. During their irregular migrations in summer and fall, however, they may be found in any habitat and have been recorded as far north as Canada and Alaska.

DARLING UNDERWING **2¾ – 3½ in.**

Identify this moth by its dark brown forewings and *black-banded red hindwings.* The brightly colored hindwings are hidden when the moth is at rest, but flash brilliantly when the moth takes flight. A bird chasing the moth might be confused when the bright color so quickly disappears when the moth alights. There are almost a hundred underwing species in North America. This one is found in the U.S. and southern Canada west to the Great Plains. Adult underwings can be attracted with sugary, fermented bait spread on tree trunks. Caterpillars of the Darling Underwing feed on willows and cottonwoods.

BLACK
WITCH
DARLING
UNDERWING

LUNATE ZALE **1¾ – 2¼ in.**

This dark brown moth has *large silvery or pale patches* near the edges of both wings. Lunate Zale is found in a variety of habitats, including suburbs, forests, and brushlands. You can see it at lights throughout most of the U.S. and southern Canada.

CELERY LOOPER MOTH **⅞ – 1¼ in.**

This gray and dark brown moth has a *small metallic silver mark* on its forewing. Most other looper moths also have this mark. Look for the Celery Looper Moth in late afternoon at flowers or at night near lights in most of the U.S. and southern Canada. The caterpillars eat crops or garden plants including beets, celery, lettuce, cabbage, corn, and carrots.

AMERICAN DAGGER MOTH **2 – 2¾ in.**

This is a large gray moth with some *scattered darker mottling.* There are about 75 dagger species in North America. This species' habitat includes suburban gardens and woodlands. It is found over much of the U.S. and southern Canada.

EIGHT-SPOTTED FORESTER **1¼ – 1½ in.**

Identify this black moth by the *2 pale yellow patches* on each forewing and the *2 white patches* on each hindwing. The antennae have slightly thickened ends, similar to those of a butterfly. The moths fly in the daytime and are found in open habitats near streams or forests over most of the U.S. and southern Canada. The adults avidly visit flowers such as New Jersey tea and privet. The caterpillars eat the leaves of grape and Virginia creeper.

LUNATE
ZALE
CELERY
LOOPER
MOTH
AMERICAN
DAGGER
MOTH
EIGHT-SPOTTED
FORESTER

GOLDENROD STOWAWAY **1¼ – 1¾ in.**
The Goldenrod Stowaway's body and wings are bright yellow, *streaked with orange.* Look for these moths perched on goldenrods or tickseed sunflowers in open fields or forest openings in the eastern U.S. The caterpillars eat Spanish needles and probably other composites.

CORN EARWORM MOTH **1¼ – 1¾ in.**
This common moth has a yellow-tan forewing and a cream hindwing with *smeared black edging.* It is found in many open habitats including open fields, suburban gardens, and farmland, and the caterpillar is a serious pest on corn, cotton, and tomatoes. The Corn Earworm Moth is found throughout the U.S. and southern Canada. It is resident in the southern U.S. but migrates north every summer. The adults visit flowers such as alfalfa and rabbitbrush.

ARCIGERA FLOWER MOTH **⅞ – 1 in.**
The forewing of this small moth is chocolate brown with *gray-brown areas in the middle and outer edge.* The male's hindwing is yellow with a black border; the female's is entirely black. The moths are found in open meadows and fields in most of the eastern U.S. and adjacent parts of southern Canada. You can find the adults perched in the center of aster flowers, where the eggs are laid and the caterpillars will eventually feed.

CLOUDED CRIMSON **1⅛ – 1¼ in.**
This lovely flower moth has a yellow-cream forewing with *patches of intense pink or red-pink.* The moths live along slow streams, in marshes, or in open fields. The Clouded Crimson ranges through the southeastern U.S., southern Great Plains, and along the eastern base of the southern Rocky Mountains. The adults are attracted to lights in late summer.

GOLDENROD
STOWAWAY
CORN
EARWORM
MOTH
CLOUDED
CRIMSON
ARCIGERA
FLOWER
MOTH

Glossary

Abdomen. The last (third) body part of an adult insect.

Chrysalis. The firm, hard case made by some butterfly larvae in which a caterpillar transforms to an adult. (Plural: chrysalids.)

Cocoon. The protective covering made of silk and other material by a moth larva before pupation.

Forewing. The forward wing of each pair.

Frenulum. A series of hooks that holds a moth's forewing and hindwing together in flight.

Hindwing. The rear wing of each pair.

Larva. The eating and growth stage of butterflies and moths; the caterpillar. (Plural: larvae.)

Nectar. The sugary fluid secreted by flowers of many plants. The principal food of many kinds of adult butterflies and some moths.

Proboscis. The coiled tube through which adult butterflies and moths take in fluids.

Pupa. The resting stage within which a caterpillar transforms to an adult. (Plural: pupae.)

Pupate. To form a pupa; to pass through a pupal stage.

Thorax. The middle of the three parts of an insect's body.

Acknowledgments

We thank Boris Kondratieff, Colorado State University, for the loan of specimens for illustrations. Douglas C. Ferguson, Systematic Entomology Laboratory, U.S.D.A., Washington, D.C., and Jerry A. Powell, University of California, Berkeley, reviewed the text for errors and omissions.

References

Covell, Charles V., Jr. 1984. *A Field Guide to the Moths of Eastern North America.* Boston: Houghton Mifflin Co.

Dominick, Richard B. et al. 1971-1992. *The Moths of America North of Mexico.* Washington, D.C.: Wedge Entomological Research Foundation.

Opler, Paul A., and George O. Krizek. 1984. *Butterflies East of the Great Plains.* Baltimore: Johns Hopkins University Press.

Opler. Paul A., and Vichai Malikul. 1992. *A Field Guide to Eastern Butterflies.* Boston: Houghton Mifflin Co.

Powell, Jerry A., and Charles L. Hogue. 1979. *California Insects.* Berkeley and Los Angeles: University of California Press.

Pyle, Robert M. 1988. The Audubon Society *Field Guide to North American Butterflies.* New York: Chanticleer Press.

Tilden, James W., and Arthur Clayton Smith. 1986. *A Field Guide to Western Butterflies.* Boston: Houghton Mifflin Co.

Wright, Amy Bartlett. 1993. *Peterson First Guide to Caterpillars of North America.* Boston: Houghton Mifflin Co.

Index